2000 PRESIDENTIAL ADDRESS

IT'S ON THE CARDS:
THAT SOME THINGS HAVE GOT WORSE

given by

BRIAN BODDY

to a meeting of the Society at the
Regent Square United Reform Church Hall,
Wakefield Street, London
on 11 November 2000
and subsequently repeated at the
Waldorf Public House, Gore Street, Manchester
on 2 December 2000

The Transport Ticket Society
2001

Comments etc. regarding this publication are welcome;
please write to the Society's Publications Officer:

David Harman
24 Frankfield Rise
Tunbridge Wells
TN2 5LF

E-Mail: David.Harman@btinternet.com

ISBN 0 903209 46 2

Published by
The Transport Ticket Society
81 Pilgrims Way, Kemsing, Sevenoaks, TN15 6TD

Printed by
Paterson Printing Ltd,
Tunbridge Wells

Index of Railcards

Introduction

By way of explanation I should mention that my Presidential Address given in London and Manchester, had to be reduced in content due to the time available.

There now follows the fruits of my research in expanded and detailed form, updated to January 2001.

Where the symbol # appears in the text the reader is referred to the Colour Section. Journal references are also shown where pertinent.

Brian Boddy
March 2001

It's on the Cards:
that some things have got worse!

I hope that I may be forgiven for using a cryptic title for my Presidential Address. It is only now that I realise that my honourable predecessor Paul Smith was equally as devious!

A considerable amount has been reported in *Journal* about the subject of Railcards, and perhaps it is time to present an overview, and hopefully, add to that knowledge.

Whilst many concessionary schemes exist throughout the land offering either reduced rate or free travel on buses, trains etc., my focus is mainly on those issued by railway operators, with one or two exceptions, but excluding London Transport. Broadly these fall into three categories. Age related, local/area residency or privilege. In the latter case I have chosen to ignore staff travel facilities.

A lot of change has occurred since British Rail introduced the first major card in January 1974, the Student's Railcard. Whilst there have been some extra benefits to card-holders, there have also been some reductions. The break of up British Rail upon privatisation has also been a contributory factor, but even under the Rail Settlement Plan, British Rail form numbers remain in fossil form albeit prefixed RSP.

Concessionary travel has certainly added a new dimension to our hobby, but where does one begin?

Logically the financial restraints imposed on students/young persons, families, senior citizens, and the burgeoning leisure industry have been a contributory factor in the evolution of Railcards strengthened by numerous promotions over the years.

British Rail certainly would have wanted to test the market place and looking back we find references to certain offers being made to encourage travel at reduced rates other than the cheap day/period fares. These are included in the text where known.

Railcards have been a growth industry in their own right. To give you some idea it is worth quoting an extract from *Journal* (89/1999).

"A cumulative total of 11,124,605 Young Persons and Senior Railcards had been issued during the 1990s, according to a written reply given in the Houses of Parliament to a question from the floor of the House one day in December 1998. Based on statistics kept for the period from 1990/91 the total number of Young Persons that had been issued amounted to 5,554,763, whilst a slightly higher number of Senior Railcards registered a total of 5,569,842. During the year 1997/98 the respective totals had been 722,524 and 679,664. During the period reviewed the greater number of cards in any one year revealed 723,524 Young Person issues during 1996/97, with the Senior highest total having been registered during the 1993/94 period at 681,425".

To detail all the finer points of availability, time restrictions, promotions, exclusions, the multiplicity of fare types, together with any other detail known or otherwise, relevant to each card described hereafter would require a work of encylopaedic proportions. Therefore, by necessity, it is only possible to give a résumé of the salient features with a cross-reference to *Journal* where pertinent.

After some deliberation I decided that a historical approach would be best, culminating with a section on Minor Railways and other operators.

So let us start our discounted journey.

PROMOTIONS
As mentioned in the introduction, British Rail certainly gave thought to promoting rail travel and perhaps it is worth looking at one or two of those schemes that pre-dated the introduction of the Family Railcard on the 17th June 1979, basically because they related to child travel.

Firstly, Companies and products.

Co-Op
[circa October 1976 to 13th June 1977 – except Christmas and Easter periods]
A travel voucher entitling an adult to take one child free of charge, obtained upon redemption of certain Co-Op product labels. Awayday, Weekend and Monthly Returns (1st and 2nd Class) and Book Ahead Economy Return (2nd Class) tickets only.

*Co-Op 1977 Promotion
Child Travel Voucher*

Daily Mirror
[circa July/August to 11th September 1976]
Journal (311/1976) noted that tokens in the newspaper could be exchanged for a voucher offering "free travel for up to two

Daily Mirror and Daily Record 1976
Promotion - Child Exchange Voucher

Kellogg's 1978
Promotion Child
Travel Voucher

accompanied children on any Awayday or Weekend journey". However, the voucher illustrated relates to one free Awayday Child ticket suggesting a variation in the offer.

Heinz
[circa September to 31st December 1978]
Upon redemption of brand labels, one option was the acquisition of a travel voucher worth £1.00 (412/1979). This could be submitted with cash to the value of £4.00 whereupon an Exchange Voucher (BR4402/177) for the sum of £5.00 was received. This in turn could be used towards the purchase of any Single or Return ticket (1st or 2nd Class) – no refund if the ticket cost less than £5.00, and no limit to the number of Exchange Vouchers used. The latter valid until 31st March 1979.

Kelloggs
Several promotions appeared under this banner between 1974 to 1983. The first was valid until 14th June 1975. Two million special packets printed and these were sold only in South Wales and West of England, offering one free accompanied child ticket. By exchanging six tokens a voucher could be obtained to validate the issue of a free ticket. Singles, 17 Day, Weekend, Economy, Day, Off-Peak, Half Day and Ordinary Returns available (1st and 2nd Class). Christmas and Easter restrictions applied.

Following the success of this promotion a general and similar offer was made valid until 12th June 1976. This time vouchers could be validated at Travel Agents.

Circa August 1977 another promotion which lasted until 26th June 1978. Singles or Returns, Awayday, Weekend, Monthly and Economy Returns (1st or 2nd Class). Including Sealink services to the Isle of Wight, Channel Islands, Dun Laoghaire and Larne.

Persil
Here again there were several promotions from 1979 (probably from late 1978?) through to 1985. A report in *Journal* (412/1979) mentioned a scheme available only in South Wales and West of England that expired 31st May 1979. Again a free children's ticket on offer.

The Heinz promotion excepted, free children's tickets were limited to two travelling at any one time.

BRITISH RAIL
Secondly British Rail promotions, either free (238/1974) or cheap travel for children from the early 1970s.

Starting in 1971 (205/1971) we find cheap travel to London on offer from Mondays to Thursdays 31st May to 10th June and 26th July to 9th September under the banner of 'Family Favourites'. Between Kings Langley and all stations to Rugby via Northampton. St. Albans (City) and all stations to Bedford (Midland Road). Great Missenden and all stations to Aylesbury. The family ticket fare being for one adult and one child but only available when the adult travelled with two or more children. Additional child tickets issued upon production of a Family Allowance Book.

During the same year, from 19th to 22nd July similar tickets were on issue from Northampton in connection with the Town Holiday (312/1971).

Also Termbreak tickets for one adult and up to two children between Derby or Nottingham and London (206/1971), repeated again for the period 19th July to 3rd September (347/1971, 428/1971) but also included Leicester to London. It was suggested at the time that this might be repeated in April 1972 but no evidence found to support this statement.

From the 9th April 1973 the Southern Region re-introduced a free child ticket when accompanying an Adult purchasing a Day Return (226/1973). A similar offer was operated in the Glasgow Area between Queen Street and Balloch Central and Helensburgh Central lines, and also Glasgow Central to Stevenston and Largs line (495/1973).

In the same year a Merseyrover weekend ticket was available for Mum, Dad and children on presentation of the Family Allowance Book. The same scheme had operated in 1972 (365/1973).

From the 6th August 1974 the Preston Division made available reduced rate tickets for one adult and up to three children to travel together. Destinations included Preston, Lancaster, Morecambe, Grange-over-Sands (345/1974). In the same year free children's tickets available from Glasgow and Edinburgh (342/1974).

In 1975, from 22nd March to 19th April, when an accompanied child could travel for just 25 pence, provided an Awayday Off-Peak Day Return or Day Return purchased.

This was limited to London and the South East but extended as far as Rugby, Northampton and Cambridge.

I have an example of some 'Happy Family' vouchers (Humberail) issued when purchasing a 'Happy Family' ticket. Valid any day except Saturdays from 18th May to 3rd October 1975 (excluding 25/8th May and 24/25th August). The four vouchers each worth the princely sum of 10 pence could be used towards admission at different venues in Cleethorpes.

It appears that the 'Family Favourites' and/or 'Happy Family' tickets schemes continued between 1972 and 1974 (346/1974, 25/1975).

In the following year 1976, an all system scheme introduced from 28th March until 11th September. Upon the purchase of an Awayday or Weekend Return up to two accompanying children could travel for either 25 pence or 50 pence respectively. Special NCR 51s were produced – BR 4563/14 Child Awayday Return, and BR 4563/15 Child Weekend Return. This was repeated in the following two years, the Awayday Return then costing 40 pence. (162/1976, 261/1977, 539/1980)

With the preamble over we step back to the early days.

MANCHESTER RAIL TRAVEL CLUB
Little information has appeared in *Journal*, although an illustration of a Membership Card current for 1980 was featured (66/1982), together with a specially printed one piece Edmondson headed 'M.R.T.C. Twosome' available from all stations in the Manchester Division to either Oxford or Reading.

Subsequent notes (107/1982) described a folded card measuring 4" x 3", numbered on the front cover and on the back details of how to book tickets. Form reference BR 34236, cover red with BR Logo and inside printing in both red and black.

The ticket illustrated here is an earlier version current during the 1970s. Printed black on thick board, the obverse covered with metallic foil, gold border and large BR Logo, the remainder pale blue with the words 'Manchester Rail Travel Club' in pale blue incorporated in the Logo. It will be noted that the annual expiry date appears as 31st October whereas the style mentioned previously was 31st December.

Another 'Club' ticket featured in *Journal* (488/1985), the accompanying report inferring the possible demise of such travel arrangements.

Two further versions of the Membership Card current during the 1970s are known. The print detail in each instance varies from the example shown, with the foil backing coloured red/gold and black/gold.

STUDENT / YOUNG PERSONS RAILCARD
The Student's Railcard introduced in January 1974 was the first of the major railcards. I have only been able to locate just one promotion recorded in *Journal* (post 1969) prior to this date. I feel sure that this is not an isolated example and that there must have been other promotions offering cheaper travel to students.

Journal (428/1971) quoted an experimental scheme operated by the London Midland Region offering cheap weekend tickets to those students able to produce a valid NUS Members Identity Card. The offer commenced 8th October, travel by specified services, out Friday returning the following Sunday or Monday. Between Euston to Birmingham, Coventry and Wolverhampton. St. Pancras to Chesterfield, Leicester, Nottingham and Sheffield. The tickets described as lilac Edmondsons titled Student Weekend with a WE overprint.

Journal (239/1974) recorded the introduction, in January, of the Student Card obtainable from NUS offices valid until 30th June. Provision was made to include a photograph of the holder, and afforded the purchase of 2nd Class Single or Ordinary Return tickets at half price but subject to a minimum fare. The Card accompanied by a Conditions booklet incorporating ten Travel Request Forms, one of which had to be completed each time a ticket was purchased. One should bear in mind that this was still only a pilot scheme and the

BR 24881 **Student Railcard**

MANCHESTER RAIL TRAVEL CLUB Nº 4600

SPECIAL OFFERS TO CLUB MEMBERS
THIS CARD MAY BE USED TO PURCHASE
UP TO FOUR (4) TICKETS

~~MEMBERSHIP CARD~~/FAMILY CARD (25p)
in favour of

BRITISH RAIL
STORE STREET
MANCHESTER
                                    (Signature of Holder)
VALID UNTIL 31.10.73
ISSUED SUBJECT TO CLUB RULES   NOT TRANSFERABLE

Manchester Rail Travel Club

British Rail

STUDENT TRAVEL REQUEST FORM

Please supply one single/return* ticket

To ....

From ....

Card No. .... | NOT VALID FOR TRAVEL |
* delete as necessary

For BR use

£...........................

BR. 24881/1

BR 24881/1 **Student Travel Request** *used in conjunction with original Student Identity Card*

BR 24881 **Young Person Railcard** - *style introduced 1st October 1982*

BR 4556/1586 NCR51 **Student Minimum Charge** *ticket*

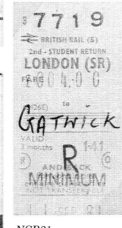

NCR21 **Student Return**

Ultimatic **Young Person's Single** *issued at 5449A No.2 - Victoria (Air)*

continuation depended purely upon a greater increase in student travel. Some time restrictions were applied in respect of travel to/from London. The initial cost being £1.65 (included VAT 15 pence).

The outcome must have been successful for in October the Student Railcard was launched to coincide with the start of the academic year.

Minimum fares continued, the rate gradually increasing over the years. Travel by 2nd Class/Standard only. However there was a subsequent relaxation. From 15th September 1978 minimum fares waived Saturday, Sundays and Bank Holidays and also during July and August. No restriction after 18.00 hours Monday to Friday came into force 1st September 1980. By 1986 the timing had been altered to 10.00 hours.

By way of explanation minimum fares split into two rates. Basically the higher rate applying to Standard (formerly Ordinary) Returns the lower rate to other ticket types.

From the 30th September 1978 Day and Off-Peak Returns became available still at 50% discount. London Saver tickets being added from the 14th June 1981 but at a lesser discount.

The terms of availability were soon amended from Students in full time education to include other students, such as nurses and schoolchildren and then in the autumn of 1980 to anyone between the ages of 14 and 24.

Except for 1974 up until 1982 all cards expired 30th September, thereafter cards were available for a period of 12 months from date of issue. Those cards valid from 1st October 1977 and subsequent years also carried a pre-printed commencement date, although one example seen without a start date suggesting a separate stock kept for cards issued part way through the year. Which prompts the question – was any reduction made in the purchase price? The basic colour of the cards varied from year to year.

Initially there was no way of identifying tickets issued against a Student Railcard – Child/Half tickets being used. A keen booking office clerk may have added 'Student' in script. There are instances where a suitably worded rubber stamp was used. However, in due course special tickets were produced with 'Student' incorporated in the text and overprinted 'MINIMUM'. Upon the subsequent renaming of the Card to Young Persons the change was reflected in the ticket text with the 'MINIMUM' overprint continuing.

INTIS, SPORTIS (PORTIS) and later APTIS issues have always included 'STDNT' as part of the validation process.

The transition from Student to Young Persons Railcard would appear to have taken place 1st October 1982.

12th May 1985 saw the availability of Savers but the discount was just a $^1/_3$ off, a prelude to changes implemented in 1987.

From 1st March 1987 (321/1987) the discount structure was altered to just $^1/_3$ off and was applicable to Savers, Cheap Day Returns, Standard Singles and Returns, Standard Day Returns and Rail Rovers. Arrangements existed to trade-in old cards bought before the 1st March to obtain the extended ticket types – the replacement taking the same expiry date as that surrendered. However, seeing that the discount was now less this was found not to be an attractive proposition. This also saw the introduction of the 'Blue 16/23' versions of the Young Persons Railcard BR 24881 and BR 4599/20 and the associated definitive photocard BR 3588/14.

One Day Capitalcards could be purchased for just £2.00 from BR stations within the Greater London Area or a $^1/_3$ off outside – a minimum of £2.00 applicable. This was replaced by the One Day Travelcard and by April

1981 Promotion - Student/Young Person Free Travel Voucher

BR 24881 Agency 16-23 style introduced 1st March 1987

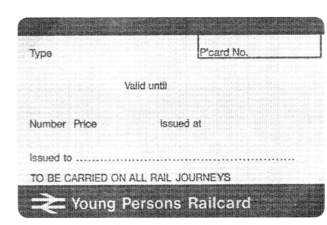

BR 4599/20 Original APTIS form

BR 4599/20 Style introduced circa September 1992

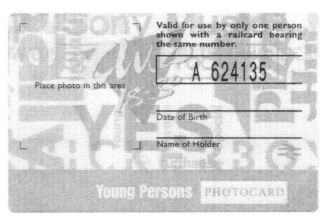

*RSP 3588/15 **Photocard** multi-advertisement style*

RSP 4599/189 Multi-advertisement style introduced 17th August 1997

*BR 3588/14 **Photocard** 16-23 style*

BR 4599/20 APTIS 16-23 style

BR 3588/14 **Photocard**

RSP 4599/189 multi-advertisemnt style - reverse

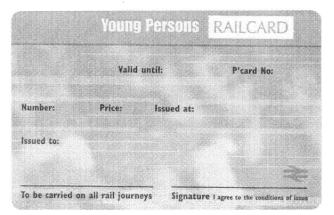

RSP 4599/217 style introduced 29th September 1998

Blackwell's Promotion Booklet

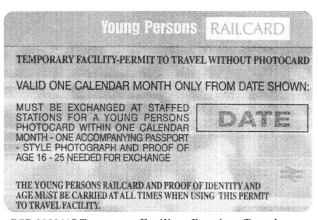

RSP 3588/17 **Temporary Facility - Permit to Travel without Photocard**

'Blinding Offers' Promotion Booklet

1993 we find the availability limited to an All Zones ticket subject to a minimum fare.

From the 1st April 1987 Young Persons were able to purchase a Network Card for £5.00 i.e. half price (321/1987), with no age limit for the second card holder.

In September 1987 the age restriction had become 16 to 23, and 24 and over for mature students. From May 29th 1994 the age availability was again revised from 16 to 25, and 26 and over for mature students.

Such is the importance of Young Persons Railcards that in 1995 a special Railcard stand was due to attend about one hundred Fresher's Fairs.

About June 1997 a new policy was introduced which enabled mature students to purchase a Young Persons Railcard upon presentation of their ISIC Card.

In August/September of the same year a 'jazzy' multi-advertisement version of the Young Persons Railcard (RSP 4599/189) was introduced. The holder was able to enjoy special offers, available until 31st July 1998, from Pizza Hut, Marie Claire, Knickerbox, Sony Music Special Products, Club 18 – 30, YES (Young Europe Special – Lufthansa), Holyman Sally Ferries and Swiftcall. The names of the participants appearing on the reverse and formed part of the security grid on the face in various shades of blue and orange. The word 'loaded' appears on the reverse of this card but not on the front. The reason eludes me. Whilst the gaudy presentation may have had some appeal it did little to facilitate the reading of the ticket validation – something that is all too common on similarly designed cards where the inking of the APTIS machines leaves a lot to be desired.

It appears that Pizza Hut was not very happy about the wording of one of the offers and this resulted in a new leaflet appearing in the September.

From about October 1998 only one passport photograph was needed when purchasing a new card.

From the 9th January 2000 Young Persons Railcards could be purchased through Train Company Telesales. A facility hitherto only available for the purchase of Network, Senior and Family Railcards. This introduced a special card for new purchasers. RSP 3588/17 PERMIT TO TRAVEL WITHOUT PHOTOCARD valid for up to one month from date of issue, to be exchanged for a proper Young Persons photo-card. Proof of identity had to be carried when using this temporary card.

By June 2000 the minimum charge applicable to travel before 10.00am Monday to Fridays was still being applied, except for travel during the months of July and August. The discount remaining at $\frac{1}{3}$ off Savers, SuperSavers, Cheap Day Singles and Returns, One Day Travelcards (All Zones only and subject to a minimum fare), Super Advance Returns, Standard Singles and Open Returns, Standard Day Singles and Returns, Rail Rovers, Network AwayBreaks and StayAways. Also Virgin Value 3, 7 and 14 day Advance, Virgin Value First, Silverlink Day Tripper/Silver Saver. Reductions also available on ferries to the Isle of Wight, Eire and Northern Ireland.

RAIL EUROP JUNIOR CARD

I have little information other than to quote from the Conditions on the reverse of this Card (BR 4524/23). It clearly states that it is not a travel ticket, and affords 25% discount "on the transport undertakings of certain countries, for international journeys made between at least two of these countries". Travel between Great Britain and Ireland excluded.

This Card was withdrawn 31st October 1975.

BR 4524/23 **Rail Europ Junior Card**

INTER RAIL

(The following notes apply to United Kingdom (CIV 70) issues only)
The earliest reference date found so far is 1974, available then to the under 21s. Offering 50% discount for travel in Great Britain, Northern Ireland and Republic of Ireland, and on

BR 4524/21 **Inter Rail Travel Authority Card**
- blue version

Sealink Ferries. Also free travel on the railways of other participating operators.

Officially described as a Travel Authority Card the style illustrated (blue) certainly current in 1977. At that time costing £83.00 for one month. By then available to those under 23, affording half price 2nd Class, Ordinary Single and Return fares on British Rail, Northern Ireland Railways and Córas Iompair Éireann and free travel on the participating railways – these listed on the back cover. (Austria, Belgium, Denmark, Finland, France, Germany, Greece, Finland, Hungary, Italy, Jugoslavia, Luxembourg, Morocco, Netherlands, Norway, Portugal, Roumania, Spain, Sweden, and Switzerland). Also half fares on Sealink and British & Irish Steamship Company's routes.

The Travel Authority Card made up as a booklet containing several pages, divided into journey sections each to be completed by the holder before commencing travel and "authenticated by the departure station or a ticket controller". Both 'booklets' illustrated provided for a total of 35 journeys, and if returned to the issuing authority within one month of expiry and correctly completed, a nominal rebate given.

An official instruction dated October 1977 stated that "blank" to "blank" paper tickets to be used for travel within these shores and endorsed IR 50% reduction. Interestingly enough a LONDON SR to "blank" NCR 21 headed 'INTER RAIL SINGLE' was reported and illustrated in Journal (465/1982, 478/1982) issued at London Waterloo (5598A).

To boost sales, purchasers of Young Persons Railcards in 1987 given a £12.00 voucher redeemable when buying an Inter Rail Card. £10.00 vouchers were offered in subsequent years.

By 1989 the discount reduced to a 1/3 for travel on British Rail and Northern Ireland Railways only and still current in 1994.

Prices have increased over the years. £92.00 (current

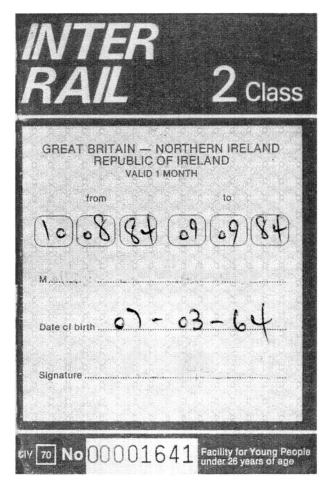

BR 4524/21 **Inter Rail Travel Authority Card**
- brown version

August 1980), £115.00 (current August 1984) – age limit now under 26 years – the brown/white version shown reflecting this change, £139.00 (current November 1987).

By June 1996 availability had been split into zones, priced according to the number of zones, and the one zone validity adjusted. Comparable prices shown for 1998 (one zone validity altered again) and 2000 noting an overall reduction.

a) any 1 zone	June 1996	£185.00	valid for 15 days
	1998	£159.00	valid 22 days
	1 April 2000	£126.00	
b) any 2 zones	June 1996	£220.00	valid for one month
	1998	£209.00	
	1 April 2000	£166.00	

c) any 3 zones	June 1996	£245.00	valid for one month
	1998	£229.00	
	1 April 2000	£196.00	
d) All zones	June 1996	£275.00	valid for one month
	1998	£259.00	
	1 April 2000	£216.00	

Zone	A	United Kingdom and Republic of Ireland
	B	Finland, Norway, Sweden
	C	Austria, Denmark, Germany, Switzerland
	D	Bulgaria, Croatia, Czech & Slovak Republics, Hungary, Poland, Romania
	E	Belgium, France, Luxembourg, Netherlands
	F	Morocco, Portugal, Spain
	G	Greece, Italy, Slovenia, Turkey and the AND/HMI (HML) ferry between Brindisi (Italy) and Patras (Greece)

1998 saw Bulgaria and Romania placed in new Zone H together with Yugoslavia and Macedonia.

Discounted rail travel within the U.K. is now curtailed. Limited to when in transit to Continental Europe. Between any U.K. station and London a $\frac{1}{3}$ discount. Special concessionary fares thence to continental ports and also through to Paris, Lille, Oostende and Brussels. Plus special cross channel port to port fares.

Currently some Ferries and certain bus operators offer reduced fares, and even free admission is available to a few transport museums. Cards are now only sold to persons who have been resident in Europe for at least six months, and are not valid for travel within the country where the holder is normally resident. A different form of booklet is now used, journey validations are still necessary. The rebate system withdrawn.

At this point it is worth mentioning some other variations of the Inter Rail Card.

Inter Rail 26 + Card. Known to be sold in 1990 in Denmark, Norway, Sweden and Finland, valid on British Rail. Available for sale in this country by 1993. Pricing became zonal – possibly in 1998. Costs about 40% more than an Inter Rail Card. Offering free travel only in zones specified. With regard to travel in the U.K. this is limited to special fares between London and Hoek van Holland, Paris, Lille, Oostende and Brussels. Plus special cross-channel port to port fares.

Inter Rail + Boat. This card valid for one month was certainly existent between 1987 and 1990. The same facilities as the current Inter Rail Card plus free travel over routes of selected Continental shipping operators.

Inter Rail Flexi. Identical to the Inter Rail + Boat but valid for only any 10 days in one month.

Both of the last mentioned cards appeared to have had an early demise.

Inter Rail Discount Voucher

SENIOR CITIZEN RAILCARD / SENIOR RAILCARD

The Senior Citizen Railcard has been in existence for 25 years and during that time it has seen a considerable amount of change in price, availability, and promotions. Sadly for some of us, the new generation of "wrinklies", are unlikely to see a repeat of the generous travel opportunities on offer during the 1980s.

The Railway Magazine reported that during the £1.00 anywhere in November/December 1981, railcard-

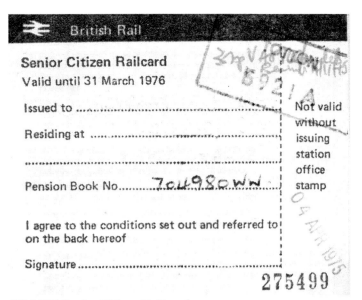

BR 24889 Senior Citizen Railcard
- orginal version

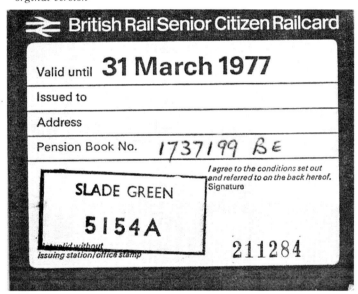

BR 24889 Second style

*BR 24889/4 **Day Returns Only** version of the third*
style. (This example has a diagnoal security grid

holders made more than a million journeys and British Rail sold an additional 75,000 Railcards. Earning British Rail an Institute of Sales Promotion Gold Award.

Nevertheless the Senior Citizen market is still seen as being of great importance and special offers continue to be available from time to time.

Drawing upon *Journal* we find in 1971 (57/1971) a report relating to a Southern Region facility introduced 10th November 1970 whereby Old Age Pensioners, upon production of their Pension Book, could obtain half fare tickets (minimum 50 pence) to any destination, provided travel was made outside peak hours on Tuesdays, Wednesdays and Thursdays. Tickets available from twenty listed stations from the Thanet area to Poole. The Tuesday to Thursday travel aspect was subsequently a feature of the original Senior Citizen Railcard! Tickets reported as being lilac NCR21s with a red M overprint.

The March edition (92/1971) noted that the London Midland Region was offering cheap Monthly Returns on specific services, again Tuesdays to Thursdays, from London to Leicester/Derby/Nottingham/Chesterfield and Sheffield.

Further details (173/1971) were given of a ticket issued 6th August 1970 for travel from Manchester (Oxford Road/Stockport to London (Euston). A lilac Edmondson with a red M overprint and titled 'CHEAP PERIOD SENIOR CITIZEN' on both halves.

It was recorded (205/1971) that another London Midland Region scheme for travel to London was then currently in operation. 3rd May to 7th October 1971 – later extended to 27th April 1972 (426/1971). From Kings Langley thence all stations to Rugby via Northampton. St. Albans City and all stations to Bedford (Midland Road) – Elstree and Radlett added wef 11th October. Great Missenden and all stations to Aylesbury. Travel permitted Mondays to Thursdays. Tickets quoted as being one piece Edmondsons headed 'SENIOR CITIZEN CHEAP OFF PEAK'.

The following year 1972, *Journal* (219/1972) stated that the experimental scheme for Senior Citizens introduced for travel within the Western Region replaced on the previous 10th January "by a new Super Save ticket facility. The Senior Citizen's Ticket facility operative in other regions continue to be available". A search through the pages of *Journal* for the two preceding years reveals no information about this Western Region promotion.

In June/July 1973 the Southern Region offered free travel to a Senior Citizen accompanied by a fare paying passenger (407/1973).

Cheap Off-Peak Senior Citizen tickets reported as being available early 1974 – no details (112/1974).

Following the preamble we finally come to the launching of the Senior Citizen Railcard which took place on the 1st April 1975. Costing just £4.00 plus 32 pence VAT. The VAT charge being dropped later in the year. Offering 50% discount on 2nd Class travel on Tuesdays, Wednesdays and Thursdays. Also 25% off certain Sealink Irish and Channel Island services.

Qualification being limited to
  a) holders of a Retirement (and Supplementary) Pension Book.
  b) residents in the United Kingdom receiving a pension from overseas.
  c) over 65 and resident in the United Kingdom but not receiving a pension.

The original Card had a pre-printed validity until the 31st March 1976. From the 1st of April 1976 a revision took place. There were now two Cards both of a similar but new design. A cheaper card costing £3.00

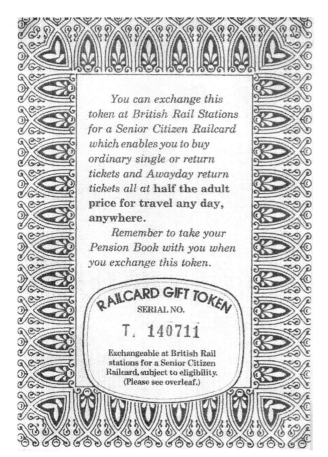

Senior Citizen Railcard Gift Token c1981

c) already hold a Senior Citizen Railcard.

1983 saw the inclusion of half price travel to the Isle of Man and child rate travel on the London Underground (both Cards). Travel to the Continent now covered by the Rail Europ Senior card. Some reductions available on Motorail.

From the 30th November 1984 both sexes enjoyed equal rights, well as far as purchasing the Senior Citizen Railcard! Henceforth the age of qualification was 60 irrespective of whether receiving a pension or not. But lurking on the horizon were changes that also affected other railcards.

A complete revision took effect from 12th May 1985. The flat £1.00 fare arrangement for up to four children continued (1st Class travel excluded) and the Day Return Card still gave 50% discounted fares. However the full rate Card now only enjoyed a ¹/₃ off Standard Singles and Returns and Savers. 50% discount now limited to Day/Cheap Day Returns. No change to travel on Motorail or London Underground, and Golden Rail Holidays. Golden Rail Short Break Holidays however, now gave a £6.00 discount, hitherto £5.00, the latter charge known to have existed since June 1983.

Shipping services now limited to Sealink and B + I, to the Channel Islands, Irish Ports and through to Dublin City Centre until 31st December thereafter only on a limited offer basis.

enabled the holder to purchase Day Returns only, the other card costing £6.00 also permitted the purchase of ordinary Single and Return tickets. The discount of 50% remained unchanged, and travel available in both 1st and 2nd Class accommodation, and furthermore travel was now allowed any day of the week.

(It should be noted that Day Return card-holders were able to upgrade to the full card at any time, upon surrendering their existing card and paying the difference)

Travel on Sealink services to Channel Islands, Isle of Wight and Ireland, and through bookings from certain mainland stations to destinations in Belgium, France, Holland, Spain, Portugal or West Germany enjoyed the 50% discount. 10% discount available on Golden Rail Holidays.

By today's standards quite generous offers.

To qualify for a Senior Citizen Railcard in January 1978 one had to be a permanent resident in the United Kingdom and –

a) already hold a Senior Citizen Railcard.
b) hold a Retirement (and Supplementary) Pension Book or Supplementary Pension (not Allowance) Book printed 'over pensionable age'.
c) be 60 or over and hold a Widow's Allowance, Pension or War Widow's Pension Order Book.
d) be aged 65 or over (men) or 60 or over (women) and received a retirement pension from overseas.
e) be 65 or over (men and women) and not receiving a state pension.

By January 1980 holders of either card able to take up to four accompanied children for a Flat Fare of 50 pence each (adjusted to £1.00 from 1st February 1981). The qualifications were now simplified.

a) persons of state pensionable age (women 60 or over – men 65 or over).
b) British Nationals living outside the United Kingdom complying with a)

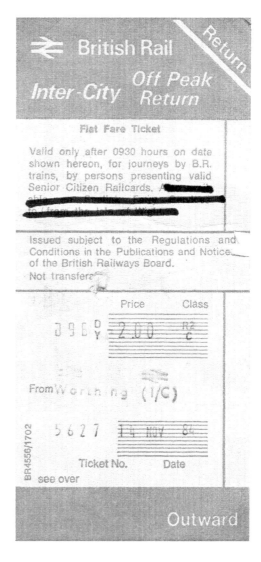

BR 4556/1702 NCR51 *Senior Citizen Flat Fare Ticket.* (deleted text reads: "Also available on Sealink Ferry Services to/from the Isle of Wight").

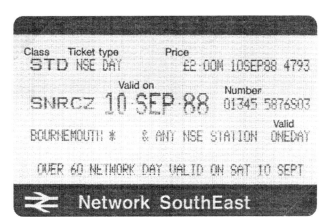

BR 4524/23 *Over 60 Network Day Ticket*

BR 4524/17 *Positive* **Senior Citizen Railcard**
*background. Style introduced c.October 1988. TV Times
Promotion issued by Merseyrail Office in Liverpool.*

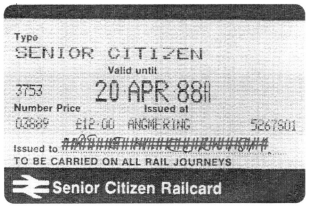

BR 4524/17 *Original APTIS form*

BR 24889 *Agency negative* **Senior Citizens Railcard**
background. Style introduced 10th January 1988.

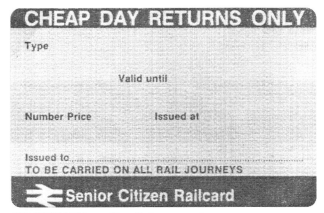

BR 4524/18 **Cheap Day Returns** *version;
facility withdrawn 10th January 1988.*

BR 4524/17 *Style introduced 5th January 1992*

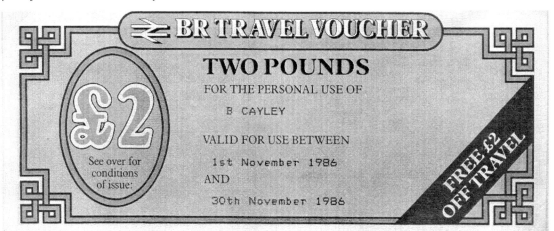

CAS/PO3668A
**Senior Citizen
Travel Voucher**

BR 24889 Agency - overprinted for a special offer.

RSP 4599/197 Issued on a TRIBUTE machine.
*Hand validated by **Babergh District Council**.*
Concessionary issue. Style introduced circa early 1998.

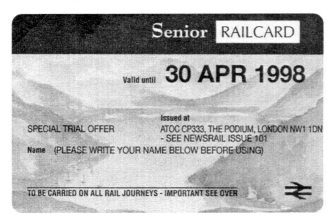

*RSP 4599/204 **Active Life Promotion** given an*
APTIS form number in error.

By 12th May 1986 travel to the Isle of Wight was limited to through tickets using the Red Funnel services via Southampton. Sealink British Ferries and Torbay Seaways offered certain concessionary fares. London Underground affording 'cut rate' travel.

In May the following year literature now showed a ⅓ off Rover tickets for either card-holder but another important change followed on the 10th January 1988. The Cheap Day card was withdrawn, and the price of the remaining card raised from £12.00 to £15.00. Travel on the London Underground now described as 'reduced rates'. Capitalcards (later renamed Travelcards on 8th January 1989) available at half price from British Rail stations within Greater London and from Network SouthEast stations outside.

Literature effective 1st April 1989 invited postal renewals

through an office at Harrington Dock, Liverpool that continues to this day.

In May 1990 the card was renamed SENIOR RAILCARD.

From the 6th January 1991 the discount on All Zone London Transport Travelcards was adjusted to a ⅓.

From the 5th January 1992 the accompanied children facility was withdrawn, together with reduced London Underground fares, and 50% discount on Day Returns. The discount now standardised at a ⅓. Discount now limited to All Zone One Day Travelcards, subject to a minimum fare. Discounts still available on 'some' ferry services. A lot had happened in the intervening 17 years – regrettably a continuing erosion of benefits.

The leaflet dated 1st January 1996 boldly adds ⅓ off most fares for through rail/ship journeys to Belfast and stations in Northern Ireland via Stranraer to Belfast'. Some discounts available on through bookings to stations in the Republic of Ireland by the same sea route.

When one takes a look at the first 1999 dated leaflet (SN99A) valid until 26th September, there now appeared a list of individual Train Operating Company ticket types. For example Virgin Value and Virgin Value First, First Great Western Day Return and Saver First etc. With regard to the Virgin tickets it added that they have to be booked in advance and that the level of discounts may vary!

Other services are detailed as a ⅓ off many bus and ship links, including rail/sea journeys to the Isle of Wight by Wightlink/Red Funnel Ferries. No mention is made of travel to the Republic of Ireland and Northern Ireland. However the second issue of the leaflet 99B valid until 28th May 2000 re-instated these destinations. Very confusing.

From time to time Gift Vouchers have been available. Those issued in 1992 did not have an expiry date. Five years later an official circular noted that these were still valid!

FAMILY RAILCARD #

We have already summarised many of the child related promotions reported in *Journal* and in February 1979 (82/1979) there was an article announcing the proposal to introduce a Family Railcard.

The envisaged scheme would comprise either a ONE Adult (£4.00) or TWO Adult (£9.00) Card. The holder would pay the full ordinary Single, Return or Awayday Return fare. In each instance up to four accompanying children would travel at a Flat Fare of 50 pence.

The TWO Adult Card enabling the second Adult also to travel at the 50 pence Flat Fare rate. Certain restrictions appertaining to holiday travel and special services to be applied. A photo-card would also be necessary. This latter requirement lapsed around 1985.

The date of introduction was anticipated as the 1st May and would run on an experimental basis until 29th February 1980. Even Cards issued after the 1st September would still have the same ending date.

The actual launch date of the Family Railcard was the 17th June, the prices of the two Cards set at £5.00 and £10.00 respectively (324/1979, 539/1980). All other aspects as per the proposals stated above.

From the 1st March 1980 the prices were adjusted to £8.00 and £16.00. Anyone between the ages of 14 and 17 (later amended from 16 to 17 wef 29th November 1981) could now be the second Adult but they could only travel at the reduced fare when accompanied by the first named card-holder.

In the Autumn of 1980 the price of each card was reduced to £5.00 (539/1980) and we should bear in mind that the validity would have been only until the 28th February 1981 anyway, suggesting a promotion.

It would seem that at this point there was a rethink on the part of British Rail that resulted in changes coming into effect on the 1st February 1981. The availability was altered to 12 months from date of issue. The card-holder was now able to

BR 24898 **Dual Holder**: original style

BR 24898/1 **Single Holder**. York CIO issue.
(incorrectly printed C/O).

the Channel Islands where a child's fare of £6.00 was applied, either Single or Return. By the following year this had risen to £10.00.

On the 19th June 1983 the cost of the Card was raised to £12.00.

On the 12th May 1985 some important changes were made to fares and discounts applicable to Railcards. For the Family Railcard this meant:-

Saver Fares now a $1/3$ off.

Standard Single and Returns a $1/3$ off.

Cheap Day and Standard Day Returns half price.

And until 31st December 1985, half price Day Returns, a $1/3$ off other tickets on Sealink ships to the Channel Islands and Isle of Wight. The Channel Islands child fare remaining at £10.00 Single or Return.

Another revision in price saw the cost of the Card raised to £15.00 from 12th January 1986.

Three years later in April 1988 we see a further adjustment. Channel Islands services now provided by British Channel Island Ferries and Condor, both offering "reductions", the latter only between 25th March and 31st October 1988.

By May 1990 the structure was further amended.

Savers and Super Savers a $1/4$ off.

Network AwayBreaks, Standard and Day Singles, Standard, Cheap Day, Day and Open Returns a $1/3$ off.

One Day Travelcard a $1/3$ off (minimum fare £2.30) – this was later qualified to All Zone Travelcards subject to a minimum fare.

A Family Railcard Office was set up at Harrington Dock, Liverpool and this appeared in a leaflet valid from 12th September 1993.

Cards renewed from mid October 1994 had 31 days added free of charge due to industrial action on the railways.

From 29th May 1994 the discount on Savers and Super Savers reduced to 20% and this saw the introduction of the Brown pictorial version of the Card and the child's Flat Fare adjusted to £2.00.

A pleasing event for us collectors took place on the 29th May 1995 when the 'THOMAS THE TANK ENGINE' promotion, in conjunction with Dillon's Bookshops, introduced the special pictorial APTIS card BR 4599/163 bearing the smiling face of 'THOMAS'. These cards were only distributed to those stations that sold at least thirty Family Railcards during the same period the previous year. No agency version was printed. Literally only a handful of Agents using APTIS machines received a supply. The promotion proved quite a success and requests were made for posters and leaflets. Stations were instructed not to remove posters before the end of the promotion, but take the names and addresses of those interested in case any spares became available.

It should be added that holders of a valid Brown Family Railcard were still able to participate in the promotion.

The other important change from this date reduced the age limit of purchase from 18 down to 16. A sign of change in our social structure? This disadvantaged existing second card-holders in the 17/18 age range. They were henceforth allowed to travel independently of the first card-holder.

At the end of 1999 it was reported that around 10% of Family Railcards were being sold via Train Company Telesales. By the middle of 2000 some 300,000 Cards in circulation generating 2.9 million journeys per year.

With all the recent rhetoric to get people out of their cars and into trains the revisions implemented from the 29th May 2000 could be considered counter productive. The children's Flat Fare was abolished. Discount now advertised as 60% on top of the child fare (i.e. Adult fare less 81%) with a minimum fare of £1.00, and all adult fares subject to a $1/3$ off. A new

travel at half the adult fare with the Flat Fare for children adjusted to £1.00. The new Cards were suitable for either a single or dual holder - cost £10.00. Furthermore two accompanying adults could enjoy half fare travel.

As an aside, a report in *Journal* (357/1982) noted that between 24th July and 14th August a West Midlands Family Railcard available for just £1.00. The card described as "green/white temporary issue valid for 21 days, hand endorsed WM". This suggests the use of either BR 24898/12 or BR 24898/14 Family Railcard Temporary Photocard Authority. Normal Family Railcard conditions applied.

By 1983 a £5.00 each reduction on certain Golden Rail holidays for up to four adults, some reduction for accompanying Motorail passengers and on Sealink services to

BR 24898/9 **Second style**

BR 4524/19 Original APTIS form

BR 4524/19 Style introduced 15th May 1990.

BR 24898/12 **Temporary Photocard Authority**

BR 24898/5 **Photocard**

RSP 4599/253 Style introduced 29th May 2000

Woolworths Promotion. Leaflet containing the two "Push Out" vouchers

APTIS form (RSP 4599/253) introduced to reflect these changes to the conditions of issue.

Use of the Family Railcard has been confined to Standard (previously 2nd) Class only. Although 1st Class travel permitted only upon payment of the Weekend First upgrade supplement where available.

The Woolworths promotion this year (2000) included two errors. 16 year olds were shown as enjoying minimum fares, this was honoured by the Train Operator's, but not the error relating to Monday - Friday morning restrictions.

It should be noted that some travel restrictions have always been applied to the use of this Card.

BEVERLEY BOROUGH COUNCIL SENIOR CITIZEN RAILCARD

I have been unable to trace any reference to this Railcard in *Journal*. Form number BR 24902 with an expiry date of 30th September 1980.

The reverse Conditions detailed specific use. The cardholder entitled to travel at half the "standard" adult Day Return fare (or half Ordinary Return fare where no Day Return available) on services between Hull to Bridlington and

Hull to Goole. Tickets only obtainable at Brough, Ferriby, Hessle, Cottingham, Beverley and Arram stations. Travel not permitted before 09.30am Monday to Friday from Beverley and Cottingham to Hull.

THE GREAT RAIL CLUB / RAIL RIDERS CLUB

The origins of this Club goes back to early 1979, aimed at those between 5 – 14 years of age. The Membership Card cost £2.00 and was valid until the end of the month when the holder reached the age of 15. Members were given a booklet containing ten 50 pence vouchers, the design of which changed from time to time, redeemable against the purchase of a travel ticket. (Some travel restrictions applied). The booklet also contained an application form for further vouchers. A newsletter formed part of the scheme containing information on events that would be of possible interest to the Member.

In 1981 the title was changed to RAIL RIDERS CLUB (229/1981), and following the raising of the Child's fare limit to under 16 years of age on the 29th November of the same year, revised Membership Cards were issued to reflect this.

In 1983 it was reported that £1.00 vouchers were also in use (355/1983), with no change to the membership fee (Vouchers continued to be available in 1990). In the same year *Journal* (467/1983) noted that a 20% discount in fares was available upon production of the Card.

By 1991 the Club had been disbanded, reputedly due to a reduction in Membership – by then the fee had risen to £5.00.

The Rail Riders Office was located in Wetherby, West Yorkshire – the address appearing on the reverse of the two Membership Cards illustrated.

Rail Riders Membership Cards
APT design

BR 24902 Beverley Borough Council Senior Citizen Railcard

BR 4402/192 *Rail Riders Travel Voucher*

HM FORCES RAILCARD

Journal (366/1980) first made reference to this Card, introduced on the 1st July 1980 on an experimental basis. The initial Cards (501/1980), having a unique serial letter reflecting the issuing branch of the Services, had a pre-printed expiry date of 31st December 1982.

Available to members of HM Forces together with wives/husbands and dependant children between the ages of 14 and 17 years of age. Later adjusted to 16/17 years in line with the raising of the child fares age limit. In certain circumstances dependant sons and daughters aged 18 and over. Affording half rate travel 1st or 2nd Class, Ordinary Singles/Returns, Day Singles and Day Off-Peak Returns. Also

the same discount on through rail/ferry tickets on Sealink services to the Isle of Wight. Not available, however, for duty travel or regular travel between home and place of duty, work or education.

Towards the latter part of 1982 it became possible to take up to four accompanied children at a Flat Fare of £1.00 each. At that time it was anticipated that the HM Forces Railcard would continue for a further two years (435/1982).

By May 1986 a two tier discount in place, 34% and 50%. The latter applying only to Day Returns and Cheap Day Singles.

In early 1989 a new and smaller Card was introduced with a separate photo-card bearing an expiry date of 31st December 1989. The following year's Card expiring 31st December 1990 and photo-card, both had identical pre-printed serial numbers, hitherto the serial number was added to the photo-card in script.

Another change in design saw the introduction of a pictorial Card valid until 31st December 1991. Interestingly these two changes were contemporary with changes in the design of other railcards.

From 1st January 1991 the Card offered a 34% discount on Standard Singles/Returns (no change), Cheap Day Returns (previously 50%) and 26% on Savers (previously 34%). One

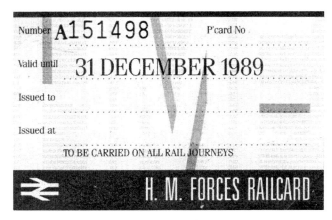

BR 24903/4 **Army Issue**; *second style*

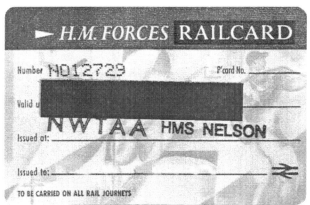

BR 24903/4 **Naval issue**. *Third style. The black area is where the validity extension stickers have been added. They do not photocopy, perhaps a security device*

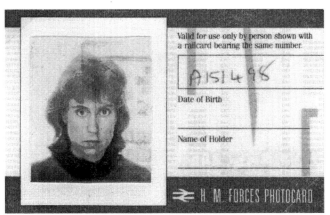

BR 24903/5 **Photocard**; *Army issue.*

BR 24903/5 **Photocard**; *Naval issue*

Day Travelcards were now available at 34% discount subject to a minimum fare. At the same time a minimum fare structure was introduced £3.00 for Singles and Cheap Day Returns and £6.00 for standard fares to restrict the use of the Railcard before 10.00am.

A certain amount of confusion appears to have arisen in 1993 regarding the minimum fare. Consulting copies of the National Fares Manuals (Section F) dated 3rd January and 16th May the former shows the rates to be £4.00 and £8.00 and the latter £8.00 and £12.00. The higher rates applicable to First and Standard Open Returns/Day Returns. Yet referring to Section K of the 16th May edition the rates appear as £6.00 and £12.00. The subsequent issue dated 3rd October quotes £6.00 and £12.00, suggesting a slight aberration. The minimum fare only applied to Monday to Friday and was waived during the months of July and August. I suspect these conditions were applied from the introduction of the minimum fare on the 1st January 1991.

A subtle change to the design of the Card valid until 31st March 1994 saw the inclusion of two boxes, one quoting the Card expiry date, the other left blank. Later the expiry date was extended by affixing a dated sticker (478/1993, 479/1993).

From the 28th May 1995 the Flat Fare for accompanied children became £2.00.

A new style of Card was introduced from the 1st April 1998, this time 'valid 12 months from date shown' including an exhortation 'security ink must be used' to validate card. From the same date the holder was required to pay a nominal fee to the Ministry of Defence. Understood to be £2.00.

From the 26th September 1999 the minimum rates were revised to £7.00 and £14.00. The higher amount basically relating to First Day/Cheap Day/Open Returns and Standard Day/Open Returns. Discount rates remaining at 34% and 26%.

The paucity of information on this railcard is regretted but one should add that the Services were and probably are still keen to ensure the recovery of railcards at the time of expiry or when members of the Services return to 'Civvy Street'.

MONTHLY TRAIN PASS

Heralded as British Rail's biggest ever promotion according to the "Grocer" 13th May 1981. A million pound scheme involving Daz, Fairy Liquid, Crest Toothpaste, Head & Shoulders Shampoo, Mothers Pride Bread, Bisto, Stork SB, PG Tips Tea, McVities Digestive Biscuits, McDougalls and Bero Flour, Penguin Biscuits and Maxwell House Coffee. Backed up by television and press.

To obtain the Pass it was necessary to collect nine different product labels and send them to Free Train Travel, Dept. 700, Sunderland.

The scheme ran from September 1981 until 17th March 1982 with the last issued Passes being valid until the following 30th April. Christmas and Easter periods being excluded, but provision was made to add the non-available days to any Passes which had a currency around these times. The Pass enabled the holder to take one adult or child free, and purchase Awayday (Day or Off-Peak), Weekend or Monthly Return tickets including ferry travel to/from the Isle of Wight. The respective ticket restrictions applied and in addition Awayday Returns could not be used before 09.30am Monday to Fridays and on certain InterCity journeys on Saturday mornings 'as dictated by the football programme'. In this latter respect I remember attempting to purchase a ticket to Sheffield from St. Pancras one Saturday. My colleague and I must have presented a 'reasonable' appearance and were issued with a ticket to Chesterfield with instructions to obtain the onward Return from the guard!

The booklet, individually numbered, having a yellow front cover with red BR Logo, Conditions inside covers and on the back. Eight pages each providing four authorisation boxes for the insertion of the relevant Booking Office stamp at the time of purchasing tickets.

Monthly Train Pass Booklet

Towards the end of the scheme it was reported in *Journal* (154/1982) that a 50 pence Travellers Fare voucher was included with newly issued Passes. Also a leaflet stating that London Savers and InterCity Savers for journeys from London could be purchased at £1.00 off tickets up to £10.00 or £2.00 above. However both the holder and accompanying person had to pay for their tickets.

JOURNEY CLUB RAILCARD

Introduced in September 1981 (318/1981) for Annual Season ticket holders and conferred upon the holder the right to purchase, at half price, anywhere in the country, 'Standard' Day (later called 'Awayday') or Day Off-Peak Returns on Saturday, Sundays and Bank Holidays. The Card costing £2.00.

In addition a second Card could be purchased, price £1.00, for a family member, or friend (14 years of age or over) with the same travelling rights, plus Tuesday, Wednesday and Thursdays. A quarterly news journal entitled "Journey" was sent to holders containing discount offers on hotel accommodation, Sealink travel etc. This was achieved by sending the station validated application form to British Rail Journey Club for registration.

The cards coloured Green and Red respectively, with 'Day Returns Only' in blue, initially had a pre-printed validity until 31st December 1982, the following year's issue valid until 31st December 1983. Thereafter a manually applied expiry date.

Either card-holder entitled to take up to four accompanying children for a Flat Fare of £1.00 each, but only for 2nd Class travel.

As a prelude to the launch, Annual Season Ticket holders were able to apply for a voucher which offered a free day return journey between any two mainland stations in England, Scotland or Wales provided they were accompanied by another adult and/or up to two children. This offer was valid between 1st and 26th July, also 10th and 31st August. Travel before 09.30 Monday to Friday and special services excepted. (A similar offer was made between 1st and 30th September 1983).

BR 24908 **Journey Club Railcard.** *Annual Season Ticket Holders version.*

By 31st December 1982 British Rail reported that Membership had reached 45,000.

The age limit for the Nominee's Card was raised to 16 years in line with the child's fare revision of November 1981.

From 1st January 1983 Nominees were then able to travel on Mondays, but a time restriction was introduced so that now journeys could not be made before 10.00am Monday to Thursdays. The cost of the Card increased to £3.00.

Other known promotions were:-

   a) Holders of Annual Season tickets applying to join Journey Club up to 31st March 1982 could enter a competition. Prize one of ten free Annual Season tickets (157/1982).

   b) Card-holders applying for renewal before 17th December 1982 received three £1.00 Travel Vouchers (BR 24907/4) valid until 31st March 1983 (152/1983)

   c) Between 26th March and 9th April 1983 the 'Green' Journey Club Railcard validity was waived for the Easter holiday period permitting travel after 10.00am Mondays to Thursdays (317/1983).

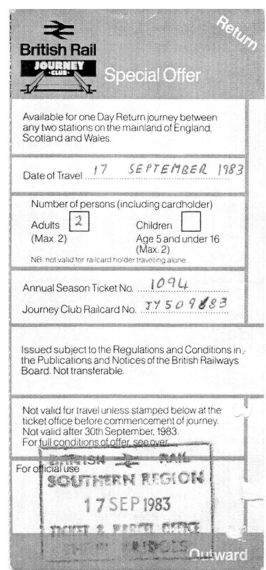

Annual Season Ticket Holders Journey Club Card Free Ticket Voucher

left: Station copy   *right: Travel Ticket*

The quarterly "Journey" newsletter and offers were discontinued from 1st January 1984. Any Cards purchased on or after 9th September that year only valid until 11th May 1985. From the following day the Annual Season Ticket Holders Railcard introduced.

As an aside a leaflet (BR 24908/7) dated September 1984 announced these changes. What is of interest it stated that from Sunday 9th September holders of adult Season tickets valid for one month or more were able to purchase half price Day Returns (Cheap Day Singles added later) for travel at Weekends and Bank Holidays. This facility ceased 11th September 1989.

FIRST CLASS EXECUTIVE RAILCARD
This Card enabled the purchaser of a 1st Class ticket at Birmingham New Street to any destination on the route to Sheffield – Leeds/Newcastle – Edinburgh and Gloucester – Swansea/Paignton/Penzance to acquire an additional 1st Class ticket free of charge for a friend. The expiry date being 31st August 1982.

I have been unable to find any reference in *Journal*.

DISABLED PERSONS RAILCARD
The first information on this Railcard appeared in *Journal* in 1981 (235/1981) commenting that discussions were in progress to introduce such a Card. The scheme commenced early 1982 (429/1982) with the initial Card being valid until 31st December 1982, thereafter renewable annually from date of purchase. All applications handled by the Railcard Office in York.

The Railcard, costing £10.00 afforded the holder and an accompanying escort half price Awayday tickets, Ordinary Singles and Returns.

From the 19th June 1983 the price was adjusted to £12.00 (273/1983). Half rate travel became available on the London Underground, including escort, from 8th January 1984, later modified and subsequently withdrawn after the 2nd January 1993.

Reviewing literature published May 1984 the Disabled Persons Railcard was available for the registered blind, partially sighted, deaf but no speech, those receiving Attendance or Mobility Allowance, War Pensioner's Mobility Supplement, Industrial Disablement Benefit, War or Service Disability Pension for 80% or more disability. Also those with

a DHSS motor car or drivers of invalid three-wheelers.

First time applicants were required to obtain Post Office approval on the application form, or send suitable documentation to British Rail who conducted a check with the DHSS.

In addition to the discounted tickets mentioned above, a discount of 50% was available on Sealink and the B + I services to the Channel Islands, Irish Ports, Isle of Man, Isle of Wight and through to Dublin City Centre. Together with some reductions on Motorail and £5.00 off Golden Rail Holidays.

From the 12th May 1985 considerable changes took place.

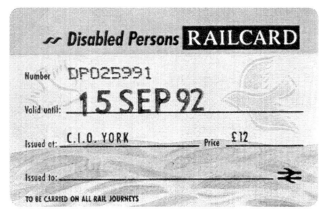

BR 24906 "Bird" design, unusually this carries a preprinted price. C.I.O. York issue. Similar design, later issues show the issuing office as DPRO Newcastle.

RSP 24912 **DPRO Newcastle** issue.
Style introduced end 1998/early 1999.

Saver, Standard Singles and Returns were now a 1/3 off whilst Cheap Day and Standard Day Returns continued to enjoy a 50% discount. After the 31st December the travel facilities to the Isle of Man and Isle of Wight were withdrawn and the Sealink and B + I fares noted as being at reduced rates up to this date. Thereafter travel on either of the last two mentioned companies being limited to special offers. The Golden Rail offer adjusted to £6.00 and reductions continuing on Motorail.

One Day Travelcards were available until 31st December 1990 at 50% discount, thereafter at a 1/3 off subject to a minimum fare.

By January 1992 the price had risen to £14.00.

A further adjustment took place from the 3rd January 1993 when the discount was standardised at a 1/3 off.

Between the end of 1995 and the latter part of 1996 the issue of Disabled Persons Railcards was transferred from C.I.O. York to DPRO Newcastle.

From 4th January 1998 a 10% discount became available on Caledonian Sleeper fares.

BR 24906 **Disabled Persons Railcard**.
Original style issued at York C.I.O.

A new version of the Railcard appeared between end 1998/early 1999 bearing Form Number RSP 24912. (The same form reference for the Agency version of the Network Card - BR 24912)

To bring us up to date it is interesting to note that currently, as a casual non-cardholder, some better discounts are available to the disabled. For those registered as visually impaired, and upon production of suitable documentation, or persons remaining in their own wheelchair obtain:-

A ⅓ off Single, First Class and Standard Open Returns
50% off First Class/Standard Day Returns

The accompanied escort enjoying the same discounts. Furthermore blind and partially sighted people can be issued with one adult Season ticket to cover two persons. Both travelling for the price of one – a different companion permitted.

Discounts continue at a ⅓ off although certain Train Operating Companies have further discount offers. Qualifications remain virtually the same. The application form now forms part of a detailed booklet and provision is made for authorisation to be made only by the Social Services or a Registered Medical Practitioner.

An interesting feature today concerns Disabled Persons Railcard holders travelling in wheelchairs. Should they have to remain in their wheelchair and have to travel in the 'guards van' they can claim a 50% refund of the fare paid for that section of their journey. The Conductor endorsing the travel ticket accordingly. This applies only to Saver, Returns, Network AwayBreaks/StayAway tickets.

RAIL EUROP SENIOR
(The following notes apply to United Kingdom (CIV 70) issues only)
The Senior Citizen Railcard literature dated 19th June 1983 announced the introduction of this facility at a cost of £5.00. Available to existing Senior Citizen Railcard holders and valid only in conjunction with same. (Quite a sharp contrast to recent years. Since 1995, no mention is made of this facility in

the Senior Railcard literature!). Offering reduced rate travel to the Continent and on Continental domestic services.

A report in *Journal* (273/1983) quoted half price travel. From 29th May 1994 cheap travel on Continental domestic services withdrawn. Any reductions thenceforth only on cross-border travel.

The first illustrated Card incorporates a list of participating operators on the back cover with discounts shown as either 30% or 50%. Conditions on the inside printed in English, French and German together with time restrictions. Commencement of journeys limited to between Monday 12.00 noon to Friday 12.00 noon and Saturday 12.00 noon to Sunday 12.00 noon.

A similar card, print dated November 1987, omits the time restriction but also includes a list of Maritime operators participating in the scheme. A later version, print dated February 1992, states no journeys within Belgium, France, Italy and Spain.

The second card illustrated now sub-titled Senior Railcard, states that discounts only available on international journeys. A list of the participating operators and shipping companies included.

By 1996 discounts now reduced with a maximum of 30% on international point-to-point fares, including Eurostar and rail connected sea crossings.

This Card will no longer be valid after June 2001. The replacement to be known as RAILPLUS, costing £12.00 and offering a 25% discount on international cross-border journeys, including both rail and sea.

Rail Europ Senior Citizen
BR 4521/14 dated May 1993
Senior Railcard version

Rail Europ Senior Citizen
BR 4521/14 Senior Citizen Railcard version

VOYAGER RAILCARD
This Card was test marketed in the Stoke-on-Trent area and launched 23rd July 1983 (404/1985). Issuing stations being Barlaston, Blythe Bridge, Congleton, Etruria, Kidsgrove, Longport, Longton, Stoke-on-Trent and Stone together with a few travel Agents. Available to any adult at a cost of £16.00 and valid for twelve months.

Use of the card required the holder to be accompanied by at least one, maximum three other persons, adults or children. A 50% discount off Cheap Day Singles/Returns and a ¹/₃ off Saver fares, 2nd Class travel only – normal ticket restrictions applying. Children paying the normal child fare.

Anybody not satisfied could relinquish their Card within one month and claim a full refund.

The scheme was disappointing and concluded 30th April 1986 after that date no more Cards were to be issued. However there was apparently some resistance from existing holders and renewals were permitted. It seems it died a death thereafter.

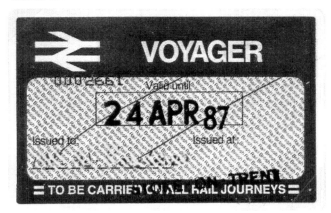

BR 24881/5 **Voyager** *plastic version*

BR 4889/1 **Voyager** *pseudo APTIS version.*
Reverse text also includes form number BR 4599/18

The card at top made of plastic. The lower card is very much APTIS in style and carries two form numbers on the reverse. BR 4889/1 and BR 4599/18. The last mentioned form number was later used for the APTIS Senior Citizen Cheap Day Railcard.

TRAVEL KEY

Journal (355/1983) announced the introduction of this Credit Card scheme. Primarily for the company executive market. Costing £12.50 per annum for use when travelling by rail and/or paying for items and services from Travellers Fare, Sealink, Godfrey Davis Europcar, Red Star Parcels and some 200 hotels covering business and leisure locations.

The Card was tendered for the service rendered and the account sent on a monthly basis to the holder's company. During the launch period up to the end of 1983 extra discounts were on offer. 5% off rail travel, 25% off the cost of a sleeper berth, 10% off train restaurant meals and hotel room charges, and 15% off car hire. Other incentives were also available.

From 1st January 1984 some changes introduced. Named user Card cost £12.50 and the authorised user of a Company Card cost £20.00. Although the initial promotion offers

Travel Key plastic card

withdrawn, some new Shortbreak and Holiday incentives added plus a bonus of one free 1st Class ticket to any BR Station on a Saturday or Sunday once an initial £50.00 spent on rail fares or services. The 5% discount on rail travel continued until 31st December for any person purchasing a Card before 31st May (121/1984, 167/1984).

It was reported (357/1985) that British Rail had to withdraw the free travel and holiday bonuses because the Inland Revenue considered them to be a taxable benefit. Current holders were still able to enjoy these facilities until their existing Card expired.

The scheme was withdrawn after 31st August 1986 (530/1986) due to a reduction in use.

CORNISH RAILCARD

This Card has gone through an interesting metamorphose since its inception both in use and design.

The Card was launched on the 4th November 1983 (119/1984) as part of the Cornish Railways promotion and valid until 31st December (1984?). Costing £6.00 for Adults and £3.00 for Children.

Offering half price travel (1st and 2nd Class) between any two stations in Cornwall and return journeys only to Plymouth. A bonus offer gave one 2nd Class Ordinary Return at half fare to any inland destination outside Cornwall or a reduction between £2.00 and £5.00 on a London Saver.

In May 1984 (367/1984) the cost of the Card was halved. This was to compensate for the withdrawal of the bonus offers mentioned above, and, no doubt also because the existing Cards would have been valid only until 31st December.

By 1986 (528/1986) the intermediate stations of Keyham, Dockyard and Devonport were included by which time the Cards cost £7.00 and £3.50 respectively. Discounts then being 50% on Cheap Day Returns, a ¹/₃ off Savers, Standard Class

BR 4599/77 Original APTIS form

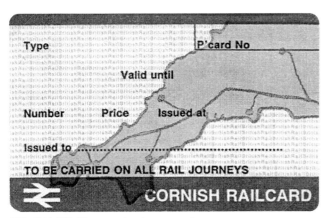

BR 4599/77 Map version incorporating
Photocard box

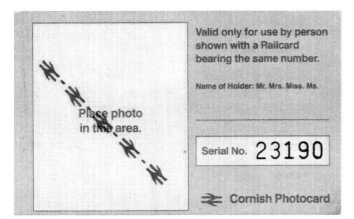

Cornish Railcard Photocard

Singles or Returns, and 1st Class Singles and Returns. Additionally reductions on Seven Day Season tickets.

Meanwhile a complete change had taken place, *Journal* (575/1991) noted a photo-card was required, discount was now a ⅓ and travel permitted on the Gunnislake branch. A schematic map (and photo-card box) now graced the appropriate APTIS card that cost £5.00. Upon checking APTIS print dates it appears that the change from common user to residential had taken place by October 1989, and the Child version withdrawn at the same time.

Currently the Card costs £7.00 giving a ⅓ off Singles, Day Returns, Cheap Day Returns (after 9.00am Monday to Friday – these tickets not available during July and August) and Saver Returns. Discounts not valid on Gunnislake branch trains arriving Plymouth between 7.30 and 9.00am.

Up to four accompanying children may travel at a Flat Fare of £1.00 each but not before 9.00am Monday to Friday.

RAIL EUROP – FAMILY RAILCARD
(The following notes apply to United Kingdom (CIV 70) issues only)
Available at a cost of £5.00 offering reduced fares on rail and sea travel from Britain to the Continent, and reductions on travel within the participating countries. Introduced 1st May 1985.

Up to 50% discount on railways in Austria, Belgium, France, Greece, Italy, Luxembourg, Netherlands, Portugal, Republic of Ireland, Spain, Turkey (European lines), West Germany, Yugoslavia and on most Swiss Railways. The same level of discount applicable on British Rail through international rail/sea tickets. Up to 30% discount on sea crossings to the Continent by Sealink, Hoverspeed, and Townsend Thorensen when forming part of a through rail/sea ticket.

Rail Europ Family Railcard

The Card available for members of a family, or group of people living at the same address – maximum number of eight. Of those named on the Card, at least three people had to travel together to qualify for the discounts. The holder, who had to be an adult, paid full fare, the remainder at discounted rates. Children between the ages of 5 – 11 years inclusive, paying half the reduced adult fare.

From 1st April 1988 through tickets from Britain only available from London. Denmark added to the scheme. The participating ferry operators listed as Sealink, Hoverspeed and P & O Ferries.

This Card was withdrawn during 1989.

ANNUAL SEASONS TICKET HOLDERS RAILCARD
Introduced 12th May 1985 to replace the Journey Club Railcard costing £5.00. The holder, second person or both named thereon able to purchase 50% discounted Cheap Day Returns. When travelling together a ⅓ off Saver tickets. Up to four accompanied children at a Flat Fare of £1.00 each. Monday to Friday travel restricted to trains departing after 10.00am with Cheap Day Returns not available on Fridays.

In January 1986 the eligibility also extended to London Transport Annual Seasons with British Rail 'add-ons', British

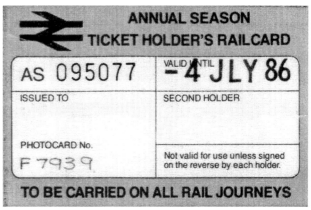

BR 24908/8 Annual Season Ticket Holder's Railcard

ANNUAL SEASON TICKET HOLDER'S RAILCARD

Type   P'card No.

Valid until

Number Price   Issued at

Issued to   Second Holder

TO BE CARRIED ON ALL RAIL JOURNEYS AND SHOWN WITH TRAVEL TICKET

BR 4599/21 **Annual Season Ticket Holder's Railcard**

Rail/P.T.E. Annual Travelcard or Metrocard. In each instance the Annual Season Ticket Holder's Railcard had to be purchased from a British Rail station. From around November, the same year, Annual London Transport Travelcard holders became eligible. At the same time there was a relaxation regarding the use of Savers at Weekends. It was not necessary for the card-holders to travel together.

This Card was withdrawn from 8th October 1988 (415/1989) reputedly due to fall in demand. Existing card-holders continuing to enjoy reduced rate facilities until the last expiry date 7th October 1989.

LANCASHIRE SENIOR CITIZENS RAILPASS
This appears to have had a very short life, being reported in *Journal* (529/1986) and in the following month's issue (21/1987) a statement to the effect that withdrawal had taken place on the 25th October 1986, apparently a victim of bus de-regulation. Being replaced by the then new Lancashire Red Rose Bus/Rail Rambler ticket (Day Off-Peak scratch card) – even this ticket had a short life and met its demise after the 30th April 1987 (259/1987).

The encapsulated Card clearly states "Valid only when used with a Senior Citizen Bus Permit with same number". Both documents required to be shown to obtain the reduced rate rail tickets.

LANCASHIRE
SENIOR CITIZEN RAIL PASS

SERIAL No. 026551

ISSUED SUBJECT TO PUBLISHED CONDITIONS.

EXPIRES ON

NOT TRANSFERABLE

Signature . . . .

VALID ONLY WHEN USED WITH SENIOR CITIZEN BUS PERMIT WITH SAME NUMBER.

Lancashire Senior Citizen Rail Pass

Holders of the Senior Citizen Bus Pass issued by any Lancashire District Council were entitled to purchase this Card for £5.50. Affording half price Day Return tickets and one third off Standard Returns or Singles, and Saver tickets at any time subject to any restrictions applicable to such tickets.

Availability between any two stations in Lancashire and to Manchester (Victoria) from Blackburn, Blackpool North and South via Preston and Bolton and from Southport via Bolton or Atherton. Reduced rate travel also available from within Lancashire to Leeds but via Blackburn only.

The passes were sold at Post Offices in Lancashire and also at Council and Transport offices.

NETWORK CARD
A Network Day 21st June 1986 heralded the setting up of Network SouthEast, generally enabling unlimited travel within the defined area at a cost of £3.00 for Adults (£1.50 Children).

Needless to say this proved very successful and was followed by a mail-shot offering cash discounts on rail travel and concessionary admission to places of popular interest. Also included were details of a 'Kids Out Quids In' promotion.

A further Network Day was held on the 13th September (£4.00 Adults - £1.00 Children) to promote the introduction of the Network Card on the 29th of the same month.

The Network Card opened up a wider market, albeit in the south-east, for more leisure travel at reduced fares.

Costing £10.00, available for use after 10.00am Monday to Fridays, but all day at Weekends and Bank Holidays plus an upgrade to 1st Class at £1.00. The holder entitled to take three additional adults all travelling at a $^1/_3$ off Ordinary Singles/Returns, Cheap Day Returns and Network Savers and

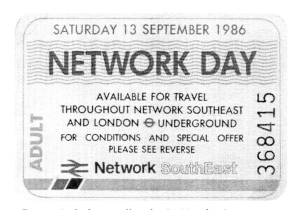

SATURDAY 13 SEPTEMBER 1986

NETWORK DAY

AVAILABLE FOR TRAVEL THROUGHOUT NETWORK SOUTHEAST AND LONDON ⊖ UNDERGROUND FOR CONDITIONS AND SPECIAL OFFER PLEASE SEE REVERSE

Network SouthEast

ADULT

368415

Reverse includes an offer of a £4.00 reduction upon surrender when purchasing the newly launched Network Card

Network Card

Number NC 356326

Valid until **20 OCT 87**

Issued to

Second holder N/A

To be carried on all rail journeys

Network SouthEast

BR 24912 **Network Card** *Agency version*

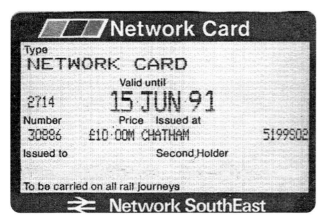

BR 4599/22 Original APTIS form

up to four accompanying children at a Flat Fare of £1.00 each. Provision was made to nominate a second person on the Card making its use transferable.

As an additional bonus, holders of an Adult Network Day ticket for the 13th September could redeem it and obtain a £4.00 reduction in the purchase price of a Network Card, provided this was done by the 31st October.

Senior Citizens, 60 years or over, providing suitable proof, were only required to pay just £5.00 (no £4.00 redemption allowed). Passengers travelling on the 'Kids Out Quids In' promotion were given special discount vouchers valued at £5.00 to exchange against the cost of a Network Card. Vouchers also appeared in the Network SouthEast house magazine, so a combination of any two of these gave the applicant a free Network Card.

Free and £6.00 (£4.00 reduced rate) tickets were issued from an office in Slough. Tickets endorsed on the reverse to show which type.

An extra incentive card-holders (and up to three accompanying adults) afforded a 50% reduction on Cheap Day tickets until the 10th January 1987.

Holders of the initial Network Card received a mail-shot reminding them of the impending expiry date enclosing a £2.00 voucher, redeemable against the purchase of a rail ticket bought with the replacement Network Card. This idea was repeated in March 1991, the voucher valued at £3.00 and valid until 31st May.

Journal noted (283/1988) that card-holders could take up to two accompanying dogs for a cost of £1.00. Was this a special offer?

Possession of a Network Card afforded benefits on subsequent Network Days. Non card-holders were only able to participate on two occasions with their applicable rates shown in brackets.

11th April 1987		
24th October 1987	£1.00	
(Ian Allan sponsored)	£5.00 (£8.00)	
	£2.50 Children (£5.00)	
16th April 1988	£1.00	
22nd April 1989	£3.00	
10th June 1989	£3.00 (£5.00)	
	£1.00 Children	
Any Saturday or Sunday between 15th September and 4th November 1990	£5.00	(a)
Between 12th October and 17th November 1991	£5.00	
	£1.00 Children	(b)
Between 10th October and 15th November 1992	£6.00	
	£1.00 Children	(b)

(a) Dates are assumed by reference to tickets
(b) Both of these are confirmed as being the product of a mail-shot that also included special offer vouchers.

Up to three accompanying adults and up to four children were also able to participate.

By early February 1990 the 1st Class Supplement had been raised to £3.00 (£1.50 Children)

The first price revision took place on 12th May 1991. A Single-Holder Card cost £12.00 (£5.00 for Seniors and Young Persons) and the Joint-Holders Card £15.00 (£10.00 for Seniors and Young Persons). Any Cards due for renewal between 12th May and 11th June could be exchanged for a £10.00 version if effected before 12th May.

The next price increase came into force on 29th May 1994. The Single-Holder Card £14.00 (£10.00 for Seniors and Young Persons) and

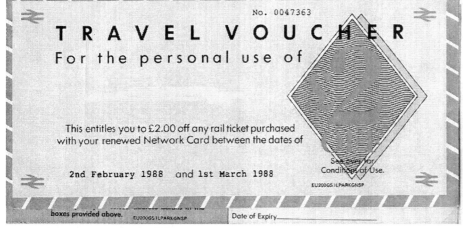

top:
EU 200GS1LPARKGNSP
Travel Voucher

bottom:
Leaflet incorporating a Free "push out" Network Card

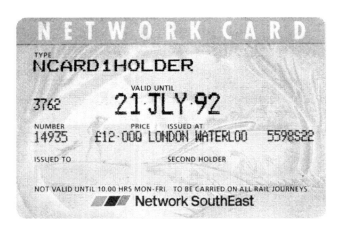

BR 4599/22 Second style introduced 12th May 1991

the Joint-Holders £17.00 (£12.00 for Seniors and Young Persons).

A free Network Card promotion is known from the early part of 1995 but no details to hand.

As a part of the 50th Anniversary of VE-Day holders of Senior Citizen Network Cards and accompanying adults were able to obtain a 50% discount between 1st and 14th May 1995.

To give some idea of the importance of the Network Card a mail-shot campaign was launched in 22 towns throughout the Network Card area in February 1997, targeting around 650,000 households. The literature contained a 'push out' Network Card valid until 28th February.

Since the inception of the Network Card the area of availability has been extended to include:-

Northampton to Long Buckby
Oxford to Worcester Foregate Street (wef 28th May 1995)
Whimple to Exeter St. Davids (by 1990)
Yeovil Pen Mill to Dorchester West (by 1990)

The Card continued in its existing form until 27th September 1997 when the NETWORK RAILCARD came into being with widespread changes, including the withdrawal of the reduced rate versions and 1st Class upgrade.

NETWORK RAILCARD

On the 28th September 1997 the Network Card was replaced by the Network Railcard and implemented some major changes to availability.

Now only available to a single-holder at a cost of £20.00. No discounted versions. A ⅓ off Cheap Day Singles/Returns, Standard Day Singles/Returns, Standard Singles and Open Returns, Network AwayBreaks and Network StayAways.

Up to three accompanying adults travelling at the same discounted fare, and up to four accompanying children at a

Flat Fare of £1.00 each. Travel availability remaining the same i.e. only after 10.00am Monday to Friday, but all day Weekends and Bank Holidays. However, the new APTIS form RSP 4599/188 (and Agency version RSP24908) was printed with a clause making reference to limitation in weekday evening travel. This was to ban Network Railcard travel during the evening rush hour. Fortunately, this was not implemented.

Any holder of a current Network Card could not add a second name retrospectively to circumvent the new single-holder condition of the Network Railcard.

Arrangements were made to mail holders of Network Cards due to expire making them aware of the changes and suggesting the purchase of either a Senior Railcard, Young Persons Railcard or a Family Railcard if this afforded better value.

A promotion in the London and South East during March/April 1998 in women's magazines was entitled 'We'd really like to spoil you'. Half of the inserts receiving a 25% discount offer against the purchase of a Network Railcard by applying to the Railcard Office at Harrington Dock, Liverpool.

By 1999 Anglia Railways became a non-participating Train Operator, but from May 2000 the Network Railcard could be used for travel on their Basingstoke to Ipswich Crosslink service. Gatwick Express also another non-participating Operator.

Currently Cards can be renewed by post via Harrington Dock, Liverpool.

(Haruspices suggest further changes in the offing!)

ANNUAL GOLD CARDS / GOLD TRAVELCARDS

Any of these tickets sold in the Network Railcard area can be included as they offer the holder leisure travel at reduced rates. The Gold Card facility first introduced September 1987 replacing Annual Season tickets and Capitalcards. Prior to the introduction of special APTIS tickets existing non-APTIS seasons given GOLD status by affixing a special sticker.

A ⅓ discount being available on Cheap Day Singles/Returns, Standard Day Singles/Returns, Standard Singles and Open Returns, Network AwayBreaks and Network StayAways. Travel restricted to after 10.00am Monday to Friday, anytime Weekends and Bank Holidays. Up to three accompanying adults and up to four accompanied children, the latter at a Flat Fare of £1.00 each. Discounted One Day

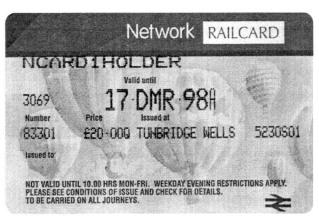

RSP 4599/188 Third style introduced 28th September 1997.

*BR 3588/4 **Twelve Month Season** upgraded with a **Gold Card** sticker.*

*BR 4599/24 Original APTIS **Gold Card***

Travelcards subject to a minimum rate. Of course, if the journey already covered by the holder's Gold Card there was no requirement to purchase a travel ticket.

In general similar conditions to a Network Card/Railcard. Holders of London Underground Gold Cards also enjoy the same benefits. The facility to upgrade to 1st Class continuing.

A sobering comment of the times. Since the summer of 1996 the South Eastern Train Company (precursor of Connex South Eastern) launched a postal renewal service – "to lessen commission costs incurred through purchases made at other TOC Booking Offices".

Only a limited number of promotions noted.

December 1987	Network Gold Card Christmas Bonus - no known details
July/August 1988	Monday to Friday 10.00am embargo altered to 9.30am.
c. March 1995	A free journey offer. (South Eastern Train Company)
c. September 1995	Reduced subscription and membership for an Arts and Music Club. (South Eastern Train Company)
16th March – 30th September 1995	Book of five 'Two for One' Cheap Day Return vouchers plus one 1st Class bonus voucher 'Free Trip for Four' (Network SouthCentral). First Class holder's enjoyed the same offers but received an additional 1st Class bonus voucher.

BR 4536/1 Ticket dated 31st December 1987

HIGHLAND RAILCARD

Like the West Highland Railcard described later information appears a little scant. Again a residential Card. Earliest APTIS print dates suggest the scheme operating in 1988, however an earlier type of Card like the pre-APTIS Cornish Railcard could have existed.

Journal (474/1992) mentioned a re-launching on 1st October 1991 and valid until 31st March 1992, at a cost of £4.00, affording ¹/₃ off Singles, Returns and Saver tickets.

An official document dated January 1996 noted that the Card was re-launched September 1994 and issued Free of Charge. Available for journeys on the lines north of Inverness to Kyle of Lochalsh, Wick and Thurso. A ¹/₃ off Standard Singles, Day Returns, Cheap Day Returns and Savers. One accompanying child enjoying a ¹/₃ off the normal child fare.

From 3rd January 1999 combined with the former West Highland Railcard but retaining the existing name.

Currently the Card costs £5.00 and the discount is 50%, up to two accompanying children at a Flat Fare of £2.00 each. The literature shows the availability as being on the West Highland, Kyle and North Highland lines.

One further observation. Examples of Highland Railcards have been seen with an expiry date of 31st December 1998 showing a ZERO price. Which would suggest it once again became a priced Card from 3rd January 1999.

Why there should have been a restriction in purchasing the Card only until 31st March in 1992 (and similarly for the West Highland Railcard in 1993) is puzzling.

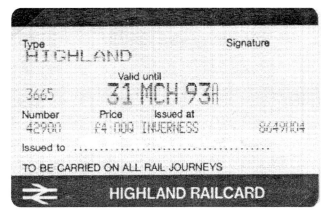

BR 4599/79 A later version omits the signature block on the front. (Signature requested on the reverse anyway). An RSP print is known which omits the BR logo

NETWORK CARD / GOLD CARD PARTNER

Introduced 8th January 1989 (101/1989). Hitherto a free Network Card was available to a person nominated by a Gold Card-holder. The new Card costing £1.00. The facility was

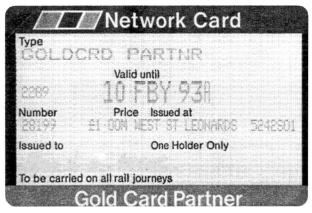

BR 4599/69 Version also exists with an incorrect all gold border

also available to London Transport Gold Card-holders, but the Card had to be purchased at a British Rail station.

The benefits to the nominated person being the same as a Network Card..

It appears once stocks of this form exhausted normal Network Card/Railcard blanks used, the validation type having progressed to 'NCARDDISCGCP'

INTERCITY FREQUENT TRAVELLER

This was a rather short lived points scheme, launched early in 1990, initial period of sale until 31st August of that year – later extended, and surviving only until 9th May 1991.

Promoted by InterCity and aimed at holders of Annual Season tickets, who since the abolition of the Annual Season Ticket Holders Railcard had been denied any leisure travel incentives.   An example of the Railcard, which bore the holder's photograph, was illustrated in *Journal* (144/1991). Cost £15.00.

In addition to a descriptive pack Members received 15 free seat reservation vouchers, together with a voucher worth £50.00 off a Dream Vacations holiday, and a voucher worth £15.00 off a 1st Class or Standard Sleeper supplement or Scottish Executive ticket.   Other benefits included the cashing of cheques up to the value of £50.00 at station Booking Offices, special privileges and discounts at Hilton and Hilton National Hotels, access to Pullman lounges.

Points were awarded to Members subject to certain conditions:-
   a) Minimum value of ticket purchased £10.00.
   b) Tickets (and Seasons) for journeys originating and terminating in the Network SouthEast area excluded. There were however one or two exceptions e.g. London Victoria and Gatwick Airport.
   c) Only APTIS or Travel Agent's tickets valid.
   d) Rover, Privilege, Excess, Group, Charter, Promotion etc., tickets excepted.
Purchasers of Season tickets gained little advantage (335/1991).   Points were valid for a period of 12 months from date credited.   Rewards depended upon points accumulated, when redeemed Member's account debited except for the first 350 points as in (a).

For example:-
   a) 350 points – Four Weekend 1st upgrade vouchers.
   b) 1000 points – Two free 1st Class Return tickets valid for one month to any destination within mainland Britain.   Out on a Saturday.
   c) 1700 points – as b) but out Friday, Saturday or Sunday.
   d) 5000 points – Two free 1st Class Return tickets plus free weekend accommodation (Friday and Saturday nights) for two at either a Hilton or Hilton National Hotel.
   e) 6000 points – One free Delta Air Lines Return ticket to any Delta Air Lines destination within mainland USA.
   f) 10000 points – A free two weeks holiday for two to one of at least five destinations within mainland USA by Delta Air Lines.

Initially it was incumbent upon the holder to claim their points by submitting their travel ticket (SINGLE, OUT or RETURN) in a pre-paid envelope, affixing a personalised sticker to the reverse.   Season tickets required the endorsement of a claim form by the issuing office.   Tickets purchased through a Travel Agent required no action on the part of the holder as returns were submitted direct to the Frequent Traveller Centre (EUSTON – NLC 3010).   Standard APTIS form BR 4599 used validated FTVIP, the same validation appearing on Season tickets where issued.

BR 4599/92

It was envisaged that the system would become fully automated.

Upon the demise of the scheme Members were rewarded with free 1st Class tickets relative to the number of points accrued.   Special APTIS forms being used

STRATHCLYDE RESIDENT'S CARD

Day Tripper Cards have been a feature of the Strathclyde Area for several years.   To extend the area of availability the Strathclyde Residents's Card was introduced (303/1992, 544/1992) to enable the holder to travel over certain sections of lines operated by Scotrail, but not supported by the PTE. Supplied Free of Charge, minimum age 16 years.

The lines concerned were Ayr to Barrhill, Kilmarnock to New Cumnock, Kilmarnock to Troon and Helensburgh Upper to Ardlui. A nominal supplementary fare of 10 pence for Adults and 5 pence for Children being charged, and in fact these rates did not alter during the currency of the Card.

The subsequent re-organisation of local government in Scotland taking effect from the 1st April 1996 extended the PTE's Area of control to include those sections of lines mentioned above so that the Resident's Card was no longer necessary and was duly withdrawn.

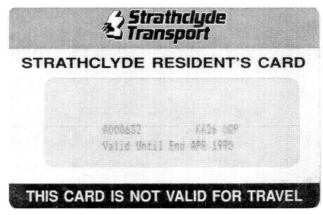

Strathclyde Resident's Card

WEST HIGHLAND RAILCARD

A residential Railcard that apparently dates from 1st October 1993.   The contemporary leaflet states that the Card could only be purchased between the date already mentioned and 31st March 1994 at a cost of £5.00, but still valid for a period of twelve months.

Limited to travel intermediately between Mallaig and Helensburgh Upper and through tickets to Dumbarton,

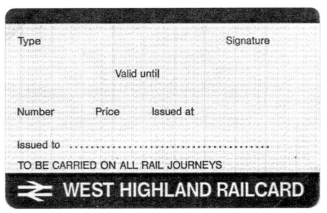

BR 4599/145 A later version omits the Signature block on the front. (Signature requested on reverse anyway).

Dalmuir and Glasgow Queen Street. Offering a ⅓ off Standard Singles, Day Returns,, Cheap Day Returns and Saver tickets. One accompanying child.enjoying a ⅓ off the normal child fare.

The leaflet referred to above also included an offer whereby the holder could submit tickets purchased with their West Highland Railcard up to the value of £20.00 whereupon they would receive a £5.00 voucher for use against the purchase of further tickets. There was a proviso that the vouchers could only be redeemed at Scotrail stations and for the purchase of Scotrail tickets except APEX.

Official documentation dated January 1996 states that the Card was re-launched in September 1994 but now Free of Charge. The area covered extended to include the line between Crianlarich and Oban. Also the residential area for qualification adjusted.

Combined with the Highland Railcard from 3rd January 1999.

THAMES TRAINS TRIPCARD

An illustration of this pictorial Card appeared in *Journal* (415/94). The free Card formed part of a promotional leaflet, of the 'push out' variety. Valid for up to two months, with an expiry date of 24th September. Affording discount travel for journeys originating from stations between Acton Main Line and Slough, plus the Greenford branch to any station served by Thames Trains, including Stratford-Upon-Avon and Hereford. Reverse conditions identical to the then current APTIS Network Card and incorporating a pre-printed black stripe.

Your free Thames Trains TripCard lets you travel for a full THIRD off the normal fare, at off peak times (i.e. anytime weekends and weekdays after 10.00 a.m.). You can use it anywhere on the Thames Trains network through April and May.

The benefits of your free Thames Trains TripCard include:-

Your free Thames Trains TripCard can be used jointly or independently by one of two adults whose names and signatures are shown on the Card. The benefits include:

Ψ 1/3 off the normal price of:
- *Cheap Day Singles and Returns*
- *Savers and Super Savers*
- *Awaybreaks (for up to five days away)*
- *Standard Singles and Returns*

Ψ Take up to three extra adults (maximum four adults in party) for the same discounted fare.

Ψ Travel with up to four children for a flat fare of £1 each.

Ψ Upgrade to First Class travel for a supplement of only £3 per person, £1.50 for children for each leg of the journey.

Three Child Day Return promotion tickets. 9006 pre-priced 25p but issued for a later promotion at 40p.

Flat Fare tickets: 7296: Family/Senior Citizen, 9630: Special Promotion, 2607: Senior Citizen

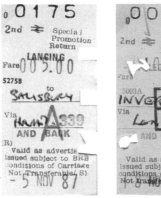

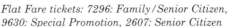

Free Child and Senior Citizen tickets

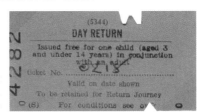

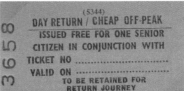

A, B and C overprint tickets used for Senior Citizen and Young Person promotions

BR 24910/3
Cornish Railcard - *Adult version*

*Original **Student Identity Card***

*BR 24903/1 Original **HM Forces Railcard** (Naval Issue)*

1st Class Executive Rail Card

BR 4599/163 Dillons Bookshop
"Thomas the Tank Engine" promotion

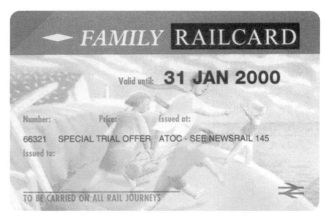

BR 4599/19 **Connex** promotion given an APTIS
form number in error

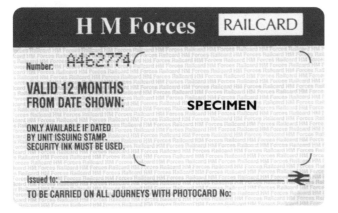

BR 24903/4 (revised 1998) **HM Forces Railcard** - fourth style

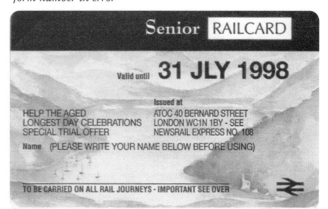

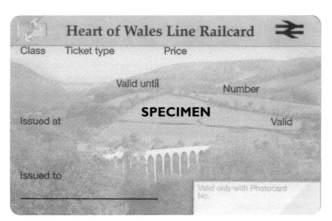

RSP 4599/252 **Heart of Wales Line Railcard** featuring
Knucklas Viaduct, Knighton

RSP 24911
Help the Aged
promotion

Isle of Wight
Island Line
**Residents
Discount Card**

**Seaton &
District
Electric
Tramway
Company**

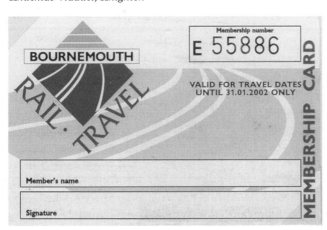

Bournemouth Rail Travel

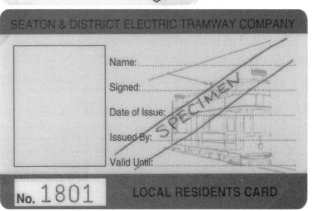

The author of the report, noted that the illustration depicted a Class 165 Unit displaying the Chiltern Line destination Aylesbury!

The promotion was repeated in the following year (19/96). The accompanying leaflet from which the Card was detached (expiry date 27th May 1995) extols the virtues of the Thames Turbo Trains, and beautiful countryside that can be viewed therefrom.

Monday to Friday travel restricted to after 10.00am, anytime Weekends and Bank Holidays. A ⅓ discount on Cheap Day and Standard Singles and Returns, Savers and Super Savers, and AwayBreaks. The same discount for up to three accompanying adults and up to four accompanying children at a Flat Fare of £1.00 each. 1st Class upgrade £3.00 (£1.50 Child) available for each leg of journey.

GREAT EASTERN –
LONDON TILBURY & SOUTHEND NETWORK CARDS
Both of these operating Units – remember this is pre-privatisation – offered a free One Month Network Card. Details appearing in *Journal* (254/1994) complete with an illustration of the Great Eastern version. The Cards formed part of a leaflet issued by the individual Units, and were simply removed by cutting and validated at stations. A printed black 'magnetic' stripe on the reverse and no form number.

DALES RAILCARD
A local resident's Card offering a 1/3 discount introduced circa May 1995 costing £10.00. (A special price of £5.00 was on offer if purchase made before 31st August 1995). No photo-card required.

Initially only available from Appleby and Settle stations. Allowing a maximum of two accompanying children travelling at a Flat Fare of £2.00 each.

Limited to tickets for travel between Gargrave and Carlisle/Wennington and intermediate stations. Also from these designated stations to Bradford Forster Square, Leeds, Lancaster, Morecambe and intermediate stations. Travel via Penrith prohibited.

Travel from Skipton, however, restricted to journeys northwards to Carlisle and Morecambe.

Journal (213/1997) recorded that a special offer for card-holders was available between 6th January and 22nd February. Maximum Return fare £2.00 with accompanied children (up to two) £1.00 each.

The ticket illustrated here bears form reference number RSP NSDR 001, an Agency version. The security grid comprises a repetition of the words 'Northern Spirit'. The Conditions on the reverse incorporate The National Rail Enquiries telephone number and a Web Site Address.

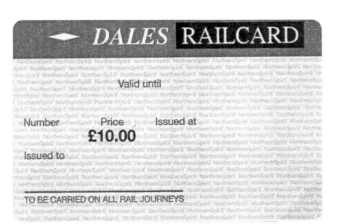

RSP NSDR001 **Dales Railcard**. *Agency version.*

SURREY STUDENT FARECARD
The earliest reference I have relates to the academic year 1995/96, and documentation illustrating an APTIS card (BR 4599/155) similar in detail to those mentioned below except that the photo-card box includes the BR logo and the words 'AUTHORITY CARD'.

The Card described as being 'printed brown' affording the purchase of Season tickets at reduced rates and issued by the Business Travel Section at East Croydon and distributed to students by Surrey County Council.

Rates known as follows:-

	7 Day	Month	Quarter	Year
Year ending 31.8.96	£10.00	£38.40	£115.20	£400.00
Year ending 31.8.97	£14.00	£53.80	£161.30	£560.00
Year ending 31.8.99	£15.00	£57.60	£172.80	£600.00

Odd period tickets issued at 7 Day rates.

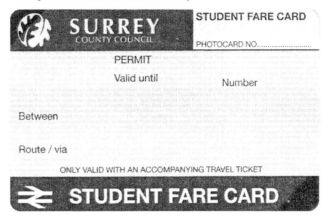

RSP 4599/254

An illustration in *Journal* (142/2000) depicted a newer version RSP 4599/234 (light brown in colour) issued by South West Trains Business Centre at Southampton, suggesting a transfer of responsibility. Furthermore the report noted that in addition to obtaining child rate Season tickets for the journey named, the holder able to obtain child rate Standard Day Singles, Cheap Day Singles and Returns throughout the area covered by the scheme.

The ticket shown is an example of the most recent issue RSP 4599/254. Comparing the reverse detail with RSP 4599/234 apart from a resetting of the text, the only variation relates to the definition of use outside of school travel.

The former states "It also entitles the holder to discounts on leisure travel within Surrey at off peak times", whereas on the later form "It also ……. within Surrey at or after 1600 hrs Monday-Friday and anytime at weekends".

The comment about leisure travel 'within Surrey' requires explanation. In a limited number of instances it is possible for a student card-holder to live outside Surrey but travel into the County for their education.

GREAT EASTERN – DISCOVERY CARD
Reported in *Journal* (305/1995) as a scratch card competition in the *Southend Evening Echo*. Also included was a Discovery Card that could be validated as a railcard giving a ⅓ off Cheap Day Returns for journeys within the Great Eastern area for any week up to the end of September.

GREAT EASTERN – HOLIDAY SPECIAL CARD
A very brief report in *Journal* (19/1996) stating that a Card seen with an expiry date of 25th August but no further details known. (Further information would be welcome).

GREAT EASTERN – SPORTS SAVER

Again another brief report in *Journal* (19/1996). Affording one month's reduced rate travel during the last three months of 1995. (Further information would be welcome).

PETERBOROUGH CARD

The logic behind the introduction of this Card would have been to fill a gap created by the former Network SouthEast train services operating to/from Peterborough, beyond the Network Card boundary at Huntingdon. No residential qualification necessary.

Peterborough is a 'magnet' for shoppers and this no doubt led West Anglia Great Northern Railway to introduce the Card. Literature would suggest from 7th January 1996.

Costing just £3.00 available only at St. Neots and Huntingdon stations for travel after 9.30am Monday to Friday (the first version of this Card quoting 'after 10.00am') and all day Weekends and Bank Holidays from either station to Peterborough at a 1/3 discount. Up to three accompanying adults enjoying the discounted fare and up to four accompanying children at a Flat Fare of £1.00 each.

Discounted tickets cannot be purchased at Peterborough.

RSP 4599/173 Second style incorporating revised time availability.

VIRGIN CROSS COUNTRY FIRST DAY CLUB CARD

Launched on the 6th January 1997 when Virgin commenced operating Cross Country services, anyone travelling on that day was entitled to a Club Card and a signed certificate.

An illustration of the plastic Card appeared in *Journal* (93/1997) valid until January 1998. The first offer ran from 1st to 28th February enabling the holder to obtain a free ticket for an accompanying adult, or two children.

A subsequent promotion (373/1997) offered one free return trip on Virgin trains either on a Saturday or Sunday during October or November. To support the claim three outward portions of Return tickets covering the same journey made between 1st July and 31st August, had to be submitted. If the tickets were 1st Class then a 1st Class free ticket would be issued. (This prompts the question. How many of your average train travellers keep their tickets?).

Between the 27th October and 15th December (22/1998) a free upgrade to 1st Class available. An application form sufficed as the travel authority, and, after use could be returned to Virgin for entry into a free prize draw.

Journal (138/1998) illustrated a Card valid from January to December 1998, then titled Virgin First Day Club Card. Pictorial with the holder's details embossed thereon. A 'Two for One' offer available from 19th January to 28th February. The free ticket comprised an A4 voucher incorporating a touch sensitive security panel to detect photocopies.

The following year an illustration (195/1999) depicted a Card valid from 1st March to 31st August. This time the holder's details printed. The report stated that following a questionnaire sent to First Day Club card-holders a temporary Card issued valid for six months.

This scheme had its own magazine (307/1999) - Issue 4 containing two offers. One enabling the holder to make two identical journeys on different days for the price of one. The other 'Two Travel For The Price Of One'.

The First Day Club closed from 31st August 1999 (411/1999), its final offer 'Two For One For Everyone' affording Members:-
1. Two people travelling for the price of one.
2. Two travel as one Season ticket. The second person being able to make one return journey between the stations specified on the Season ticket.
3. One person could travel twice. Both tickets covering the same journey, but could be used on different days.

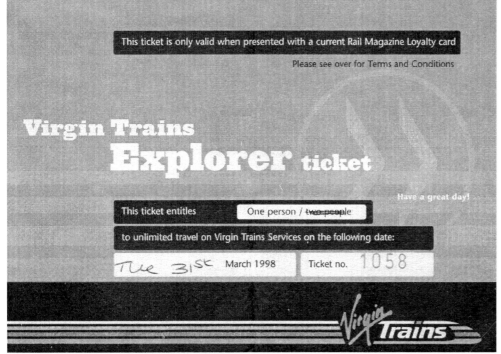

Rail Nagazine Loyalty Card promotion Explorer Ticket (red/black)

RAIL READERS LOYALTY CARD

An early photo-card valid until 31st August 1997 is illustrated together with the current version. A joint promotion initially with Intercity, later Virgin Trains and 'Rail' Magazine.

Very little has appeared in *Journal*. A Card was illustrated (373/1997) valid until August 1998 – now with the Virgin Trains title, costing £4.95, affording the purchase of Day Rover tickets for travel on Virgin Trains on selected dates and upgrades to 1st Class on selected weekdays during January and June plus 'other offers'. In November (461/1997) a One Day Virgin Explorer ticket was available, costing £20.00. In March 1998 a similar ticket was on offer (177/1998). This time a special card ticket used, hitherto A4 'letters' had sufficed.

By 2000 the price of the Card had risen to £7.50 valid from 1st February to 31st December. Offers during the year as follows:-

6th – 31st March	Two For One – Day Return, Saver and Super Saver. Accompanying passenger free.
June – July	One Day Freedom ticket £30.00. Same fare for accompanying passenger.
7th August – 3rd September	First Class Upgrade £15.00 return. Off-peak travel only. Trains arriving London before 10.00am and departing London between 3.30pm and 7.00pm excluded.
11th September – 18th October	Two For One (same as above).
2nd – 27th October	First Class Upgrade (same as above).
November – December	One Day Freedom ticket (same as above), and a competition with a chance to win two 1st Class tickets.

MIDLAND BANK FOUR YEAR STUDENT RAILCARD

This Card came into being on the 7th July 1997, available to any first year university student who opened a Midland Bank account. Issued free of charge, supported by a radio and national press campaign, messages on cash machines and Student Fresher's Fairs. It was estimated that 40,000 students would take up the offer.

Colour similar to the normal Young Person's Railcard and enjoying the same benefits and conditions. Incorporating a maximum termination date of 30th June 2002, printed below the actual expiry date.

The Bank being responsible for issue and control.

Form number RSP 24881/5. Interestingly the Voyager Card was numbered BR 24881/5 – an example of duplication.

This promotion continues as later versions of this Card exist with the HSBC tile and valid until 31st July 2004. Recent literature offers either £50.00 cash or the Railcard with acceptance by the 31st October 2000.

Original version showing a maximum validity until 30th June 2002

ESK VALLEY RAILCARD

A residential railcard offering a 1/3 off Standard Single, Day/Cheap Day Returns and Savers for journeys between Whitby and Great Ayton and intermediately, also to stations between Great Ayton and Middlesbrough. Plus a $^1\!/_3$ off Return tickets on the North Yorkshire Moors Railway between Pickering and Grosmont, and through tickets to Pickering. Allowing a maximum of two accompanying children at a Flat Fare of £2.00 each.

Discount also available on the Tees Day Ranger. Introduced circa April/May 1997 and costing £10.00. (An introductory offer of £5.00 for any Card bought before 1st July)

Conditions on the reverse incorporate the telephone numbers of The National Rail Enquiries and North Yorkshire Moors Railway.

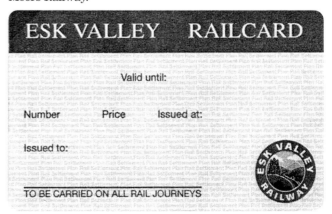

RSP 4599/183 **Esk Valley Railcard**

ISLE OF WIGHT DISCOUNT CARD

Introduced in 1997. Available either as a Single-holder version (£5.00), or Family version (£7.50). Valid for one year, the same card suffices for either with provision to indicate type.

It will be seen that the Card shows a photo-card prefix 'IL' suggesting a customised version. However, when this particular Card was issued it was accompanied by a standard RSP 3588/9 photo-card.

The Card affords a 40% discount on Single and Day Return fares on 'The Island Line'. Monday to Friday travel limited to after 10.00am, no restriction at Weekends or Bank Holidays. Minimum age 16 years or over, with a named second card-holder facility.

The Family version requires at least one child to accompany the named holder(s). In addition, to the card-holder(s), up to a maximum of two accompanying adults and four children can enjoy reduced fares.

As an aside, the Island Authorities provide a free of charge card, that does not need renewal, to residents 60 years and over, enabling half rate travel on the Island's buses and trains.

SOUTH WEST TRAINS GOLD SERVICE

From 1997 holders of South West Trains issued Annual Gold Cards have been able to obtain six free travel tickets per annum for use at Weekends under the title of 'Gold Service' (334/1997, 266/1999). Additionally off-peak tickets can be purchased at a ⅓ discount, also for up to three accompanying adults. Plus a maximum of four accompanying children at a Flat Fare of £1.00 each.

Also a Gold Card Network Card for a partner/friend for £1.00.

SOUTH KENT COLLEGE DISCOUNT CARD

A local Card introduced on a trial basis for students aged 19 years and over attending courses at campuses at Ashford, Dover, and Folkestone. An encouragement for those just attending courses for two or three days a week.

The original operational dates were from 8th September 1997 to 3rd July 1998. Offering a 34% discount off Standard and Cheap Day Singles plus Standard and Cheap Day Returns for journeys to/from Ashford International, Dover Priory and Folkestone Central on Connex South Eastern services east of a line bounded by Strood, Swanley, Otford, Sevenoaks, Tonbridge and Ashford International. No time restriction was applied.

South Kent College, the issuing authority, added their own stricture to the National Conditions of Carriage. Whilst using the Local Rail Discount Card students were subject to the Code of Conduct set out in South Kent Colleges' Disciplinary Procedure and any breaches thereof would be dealt with in the same way as if such breaches occurred on College premises.

A recent enquiry suggested this Card did not survive very long.

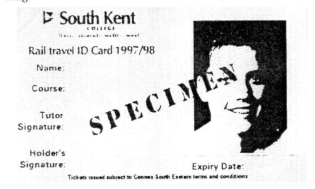

ƒ GREAT EASTERN – WEEKEND TRAVEL PASS

An illustration appeared in *Journal* (104/1998) valid from 1st January until 31st December 1998. Issued to Annual Season ticket holders affording free Weekend travel on all ƒ Great Eastern services for themselves and a companion.

The holder issued with two plastic cards. The Companion Card, although transferable, required the person to accompany the Season ticket holder. If two or more accompanying children, the first covered by the Companion Card, the others charged £1.00 each.

The scheme was repeated in 1999 (102/99). This time only one Card issued suitably styled 'Annual Season Ticket and Companion Card'.

CENTRAL TRAINS – MATCHMAKER CARD

Between 2nd January and 30th April 1998 this discount Card offered to Season ticket holders travelling between Shrewsbury and Wolverhampton, and intermediate stations (177/1998).

Validity of the Card being the same as the Season holders enabling an accompanying person to purchase 50% discount Cheap Day Return fares between any station on the Wolverhampton to Chester Line.

The Matchmaker card-holder able to purchase similarly half price discounted tickets for that section of line not covered by their Season.

NEW DEAL

Introduced 24th May 1998 (221/1998, 256/1998, 265/1998) as part of the Government's 'Welfare to Work Programme'. Issued by the Employment Service mostly through local Job Centres.

Available to the unemployed 18 – 24 year olds claiming Jobseeker Allowance for six months or more and/or early entrants to 'New Deal' (including those getting National Insurance credits only).

Maximum validity 3 months, period determined by issuing officer. An illustration of the Card appeared in *Journal* (369/1998) – RSP 24909.

Limited to Train Companies in England and Wales, London Transport and some Passenger Transport Executives. Basic discount being 50%. London Transport, Docklands Railway and London Travelcards at Child rate. Exceptions include special offers, excursions, charters, Rover tickets etc.

In passing it would be pertinent to comment that a concessionary Job Seeker card was introduced 15th September 1997 for travel on Sheffield Trams and this was replaced from 5th January 1998 by a New Deal card. Job Centres again being responsible for issue (459/1997, 183/1998).

In July 2000 it was reported that some 54,000 New Deal Railcards had been issued and that the scheme was to continue for another two years.

Different arrangements apply in Scotland with an earlier introduction date of 6th April 1998.

For those people attending an interview a free travel voucher issued by the Job Centre. Validity the same as Standard Class Day Return tickets, and only on Scotrail services. Two types of voucher exist. Basically of the same design except that one version includes the Strathclyde logo for use within that Region.

Where a person gained full employment under the scheme, a photo-identity Railcard issued, valid for six months, enabling the holder to purchase 7 day Season tickets only at 50% discount. Available for use on Scotrail, Virgin and GNER services as defined below.

a) Between any two stations Inverness - Kyle of Lochalsh/Wick/Thurso.
b) Between any two stations Crianlarich - Oban/Mallaig.
c) Between any two stations in the Strathclyde Passenger Transport area.
d) Any journey up to 60 minutes approximate duration outwith the above.

I have found a reference to a similar scheme introduced 5th January 1998 which states that a 'discount' card issued, again enabling the purchase of 50% discounted 7 day Seasons. The area covered being as follows:-

a) Dundee – Montrose/Perth/Kirkcaldy.
b) Perth and Stirling – Blair Atholl/Dundee.
c) Montrose/Arbroath and Aberdeen/Dundee.
d) Pitlochry/Dunkeld and Stirling/Dundee/Aviemore.

ANGLIA COMMUTER CLUB
A personal service scheme introduced in December 1998 for regular commuters with a direct one month debit payment option. Enabling the purchase of The Anglia Railways All Trains Pass valid for three months, exclusive to Club members – cheaper than normal commuter fares. Free seat reservations on trains to and from London, compensation paid if train delayed by 30 minutes or more. Postal and telephone service for acquiring tickets, plus promotional offers.

Membership Card incorporates a scanned photograph of the holder and the All Trains Pass generated by computer. An illustration has appeared in *Journal* (206/2000).

RADIO TIMES 'GET UP & GO' CARD
Reference to this Card has only come to light in official documentation.

Available only on services operated by Wales & West and Valley Lines, with a validity from 1st March to 1st December 1999. Basically a 'Two for One' promotion. The Card holder travelling free provided they accompanied by another person who had purchased either a non-discounted Super Saver, or

non-discounted Cheap Day Return. Due to the Eclipse travel was not permitted between 30th July and 23rd August west of Bristol Temple Meads to Penzance and all associated branches including those to Exmouth and Barnstaple.

VALLEY LINES SENIORS RAILCARD
Another product of the privatised railway, introduced 30th May 1999. Costing £5.00 enabling the holder to purchase Cheap Day Return fares at a 50% discount on Valley Lines services.

From circa February 2000 bona fide residents of Rhondda Cynon Taff or Merthyr Tydfil have been able to purchase the Card for just £4.00. The validity has subsequently been extended to cover the Wales & West services between Cardiff and Pontyclun.

Sold only at Valley Lines staffed stations.

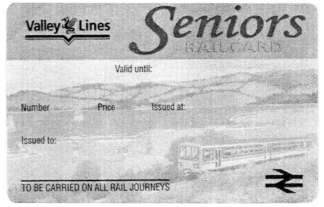

RSP 4599/206

VALLEY LINES STUDENT RAILCARD
Introduced in 1999 (May/September?), costing £9.00, enabling the holder to purchase Cheap Day Returns at a discount of

RSP 4599/216

25%, or 10% off Season tickets. Again limited to Valley Lines services, and sold only at a limited number of Valley Lines staffed stations.

PRISM WEEKEND PASS

Introduced early 1999, issued free of charge to LTS (c2c) Annual Season ticket holders affording free travel at Weekends and Bank Holidays and additionally on all other PRISM owned train operator's services (West Anglia Great Northern, Wales & West, and Valley Lines).

One accompanying adult, and up to four accompanying children travelling at a Flat Fare of £5.00 and £1.00 each respectively.

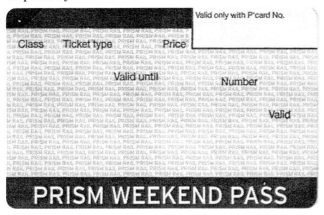

RSP 4599/244

ƒ GREAT EASTERN – SUMMER SAVER CARD

Reported and illustrated in *Journal* (411/1999). A promotion valid between 10th July and 30th September 1999.

Facililities offered:-

a) ⅓ off Family travel that included up to four children, the latter paying a Flat Fare of £2.00 each, within the ƒ Great Eastern area.

b) GroupSave allowing four adults to travel for the price of two. Offer also available on services from London operated by Chiltern, LTS Rail, Thameslink, WAGN and Midland Main Line – the latter between Luton and Market Harborough.

c) Seniors given a ⅓ off travel within the ƒ Great Eastern area.

As an aside, this ticket was advertised (354/1999) on the reverse of ƒ Eastern National and ƒ Thamesway Wayfarer tickets and, surprisingly, Arriva (Southend). Needless to say the latter was withdrawn rather rapidly!

ƒ GREAT EASTERN - DESTINATION WEEKEND

Introduced during 2000 to replace the former Weekend Travel Pass, again only available to Annual Season ticket holders, affording free travel on ƒ Great Eastern services at Weekends and Bank Holidays. An illustration of the pictorial card has appeared in *Journal* (47/2000).

The card-holder received an initial set of six vouchers valid until 31st March (further sets supplied thereafter) comprising three different types.

a) Companion - free travel for one adult.

b) Family - free travel for one adult and up to four children.

c) Free travel for up to four children.

In each instance only valid for travel accompanied by the Destination Weekend card-holder.

The scheme has continued in 2001.

HEART OF WALES LINE RAILCARD #

A local resident's Card introduced circa May 2000, featuring a pictorial APTIS depicting the Knucklas Viaduct near Knighton.

Costing £3.00 and requiring a photo-card (standard RSP 3588/9 used), currently only available from Llandrindod Wells Travel Centre.

The purchase of tickets is restricted to travel between Swansea and Shrewsbury on the 'Heart of Wales Line'. A ⅓ off Standard Day Singles/ Returns, Saver and Cheap Day Returns although the latter are not available in July or August.

The literature includes a caveat that restrictions may occasionally be necessary at periods of high demand. Details being displayed at Llandrindod Wells. This comment is not particularly helpful knowing that during the time of the Annual Royal Welsh Show at Builth Wells there have been capacity problems on the line. Due to the poor road access many people use the train but they do not necessarily all travel from Llandrindod Wells!

CONNEX LOYALTY CARD

Inclusion of this item is perhaps debatable. Reported and illustrated in *Journal* (370/2000). Requiring the Card to be stamped after the purchase of individual tickets (Cheap Day Singles/Returns, One Day Travelcards, Pricebuster, Network AwayBreaks/StayAways, 7 Day tickets and Seasons). Upon reaching a total of twelve one further validation entitled two adults and up to four children to travel together on any off-peak Connex service for one day in Standard Class accommodation free of charge.

Valid from 69 Connex South Eastern stations, minimum age for card-holders 16 years. Although no period of validity shown one Condition stated "Connex reserves the right to cancel this offer without notice or reason. Card holders will then have 28 days in which to redeem completed cards".

MIDLAND MAIN LINE SEASON TICKET HOLDERS

Introduced during the latter part of 2000, holders of Season tickets valid for one month or more are currently able to travel anywhere on the Midland Main Line network together with a companion and up to two children free of charge at Weekends or Bank Holidays.

Preserved Railways and Others

Finally, we must take a look at the preserved railway scene and others. You will already be aware from reading *Journal* that certain operators offer local resident's cards and one or two examples have been illustrated.

Members of such organisations also enjoy privileges. This might range from free parking at the Bluebell Railway for Members of the Bullied Society through to reduced rates of travel, or free travel if you are an Associate Member of the Leighton Buzzard Narrow Gauge Railway Society. Whilst Membership Cards may not be considered as 'Railcards' in the true sense, I do feel they should be considered to broaden our knowledge and perhaps worthy of inclusion in our collections. After all they have to be produced to establish the holder's entitlement, and it is surprising to see how some have evolved in design. A few examples are included in this section and I leave this proposition to your judgement.

BLUEBELL RAILWAY

The first Card illustrated has some interesting features. It was the result of the Railway's deliberate attempt to recreate the style of a Southern Railway Season ticket, and incorporates a route map on the reverse.

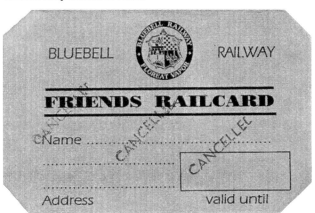

black print on dark green card

Introduced in 1994 at a cost of £2.00, valid for three years and affording the holder a 50% discount on fares (232/1995). The purchase price has only recently been increased to £5.00.

The second Card is in the most recent style and has a nice intaglio of 'Birch Grove'. The reverse now makes provision for the holder's address and the Company title and address.

I am informed that the Friends Railcard has been a very successful product.

Golden Arrow, Santa trains, other special services and the East Grinstead bus link are excluded.

An occasional offer has been made to Friends Railcard holders at Christmas time. For example from 26th December 1996 to 31st January 1997 a card-holder and their guests were able to travel at half fare with accompanying children paying just £1.00.

The reverse of a Membership Card valid until 31st December 1991 is shown. Condition 2 "Unlimited travel at a reduced rate 3rd class, on normal time-tabled trains." Life Members have a Free Pass.

black print on light green card

PRIVILEGES

1. Training for and service on the voluntary operating staff.

2. Unlimited travel at a reduced rate 3rd class, on normal timetabled trains.

3. Free admission to the stations, museum, and loco-motive running sheds, during normal opening times.

4. Free copy of the Society quarterly magazine, *Bluebell News*.

5. 10% reduction on selected bookshop items.

6. Reduced rate lineside photo permits.

Membership Card reverse - blue print

EAST LANCASHIRE LIGHT RAILWAY COMPANY

This ticket featured in Paul Smith and Brian Hughes excellent TTS publication Greater Manchester 1998-1999. An earlier report appeared in *Journal* (270/1994), described as a "Residents Annual Season ticket".

EAST LANCASHIRE LIGHT RAILWAY CO. LTD.

Residents Permit

Expiry Date (CANCELLED)

Allows half price travel for the holders personal use on Saturdays

Name (SPECIMAN) 2000

Address

red/black print

The card costs £3.00 and is valid for one year. Affording half price travel on Saturdays, but from around April 2000 this now includes Sunday travel.

I am informed that a new Card will be produced to reflect this change and some consideration is being given to possible enhancements to the availability.

ISLE OF WIGHT STEAM RAILWAY
This Railway uses a voucher system in conjunction with a Membership Card enabling the acquisition of three free travel tickets per annum.

An example of the voucher document, partially used, is shown. Each voucher numbered and perforated. The document clearly defines terms of use and incorporates the general exclusion noted on other Cards, namely Special Events and Santa Specials.

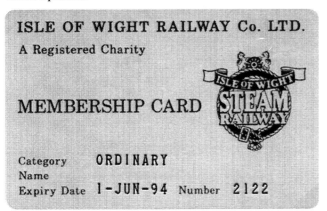

yellow plastic card; green/black print

black print, white label, yellow card

KEIGHLEY & WORTH VALLEY RAILWAY
The first report of a Residential Railcard appeared in *Journal* as early as 1988 (320/88) noting the introduction from 26th May the previous year, and accompanied by an illustration. Entitling the holder, spouse and children to travel at the cheaper fares applicable to the diesel rail-bus service.

Since then the format of the Railcard has altered. The latest version is shown. The previous version was identical except that it was printed on 'glazed' card. Unfortunately this made it difficult to inscribe the holder's personal details.

Issue continues to be free of charge with a validity of two years. Currently the holder must be at least 16 years of age and is entitled to reduced fares as shown in the Resident's Railcard fare-table. These roughly equate with the peak rate bus fares in the Worth Valley, and up to three accompanied children between 5 and 15 years of age at half price. Special services excluded.

The qualifying residency area was originally based on the watershed of the River Worth with some adjustment. However this was found a little unsuitable and now postcodes BD 21 and BD 22 are the determinates.

The opportunity is also taken to look at the reverse of a Life Membership Card valid until December 1996. You will note that provision is made to record the Member's three complimentary day tickets, and the conditions provide for half rate travel thereafter – qualified that special trains possibly surcharged.

The Company consider the Card to be a good public relations exercise. A thank you to the local residents and makes them feel like stake-holders in the railway. Also that the railway is a genuine transport resource.

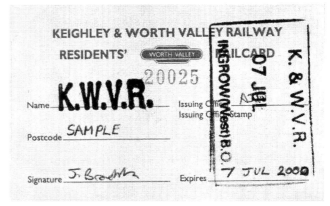

red print, pale yellow card

black print, pale yellow card

KENT & EAST SUSSEX RAILWAY

It has been established that no Resident's Card exists.

However, we can have a look at a Travel Card and a Membership Card. Both Cards enable privilege rate tickets to be purchased and also obtain five free third class tickets per annum.

Only the former defines the offer of privilege travel "in conjunction only with a valid Tenterden Railway Company Ltd Membership Gold Card". Both Cards have five boxes on the reverse to facilitate the recording of free tickets.

Issue of free tickets has now been reduced to three, one 1st and two 3rd Class.

green/black print

red/black print

LEIGHTON BUZZARD NARROW GAUGE RAILWAY

The Associate Member's Card illustrated clearly defines free travel available to the holder.

black print, yellow card

NORTH YORKSHIRE MOORS RAILWAY

Now for something a little different. Here we see illustrated two Resident's Cards available only on a Monday and for travel by specified trains. The answer to this apparent puzzle is quite simple, although I have to admit that I was only made aware of the answer during the course of a conversation with the Railway. Monday is market day in Pickering. Market Day tickets were a feature of railways years ago and it is nice to know that something similar exists today. The cards have been in existence for just over a year. Issued Free of Charge and the holder enjoys free travel. The holder's photograph being affixed to the left-hand side.

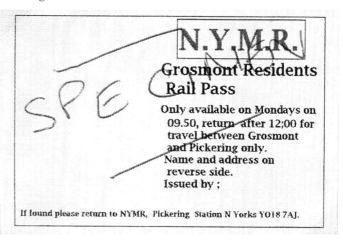

green/black print on pale yellow card

RHEILFFORDD ERYRI /
WELSH HIGHLAND RAILWAY (CAERNARFON)

This Card was launched with an advertisement in *The Daily Post* and a bargain fare of £1.00 for the period 4 – 8th April 1998. A description and illustration appearing in *Journal* the following month (197/1998). Issued Free of Charge entitling the holder to quarter rate travel.

Valid until the end of the railway's seasonal operation, 8th November 1998. However, the Card included an invitation for the holder to renew for a further five years at a cost of £2.00. By doing so the same discount rate could also be obtained on Rheilffordd Ffestiniog.

The card has now been superseded by the new joint Ffestiniog/Welsh Highland version.

RHEILFFORDD FFESTINIOG

The first report of a Resident's Railcard appeared in *Journal* some time ago (307/1987).

The Company was aware that "tourist" fares would be a deterrent for locals wishing to use the line for "normal"

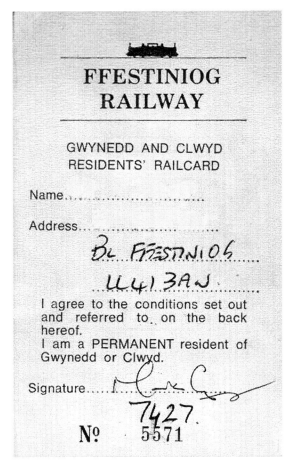

green print - second style

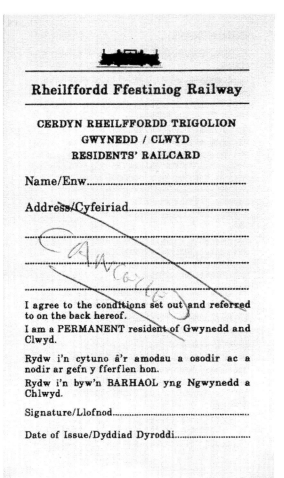

blue print - third style

blue print, black serial number - fourth style

	CONDITIONS	
5	This card should be signed on the face immediately on receipt. When so signed, its production entitles the holders personally to obtain admission to any meeting of the Society and to claim such travel concessions on the Ffestiniog and Tal-y-Llyn Railways as these companies from time to time allow, subject to their rules and conditions applicable to fare-paying passengers. Members' tickets must be obtained before each journey or as directed.	6
4		7
3		8
2	*If this card is lost the Membership Secretary should be informed immediately* **ANDREW PRICE**	9
1	50 Thistle Downs, Tewkesbury, Gloucestershire GL20 8RE **PLEASE QUOTE MEMBERSHIP CARD No. WHEN WRITING**	10
	P1 P2 P3	

black print - pale blue card; ticket control numbers 1-10 and P1-P3 on reverse of Membership Card

transport purposes. Thus the Card was born.

Initially the card cost £1.00 for one year, four further annual renewals at no extra charge, available to anyone 5 years or over and a permanent resident in Gwynedd or Clwyd. Affording quarter rate 3rd Class travel, an accompanying child travelling fee of charge.

Since the original card, illustrated in *Journal* (564/1988), some design changes, three versions known, have taken place and these are now discussed.

a) Provision on the inside for a passport photograph and yearly endorsements.

b) Complete re-design with bi-lingual text. Conditions revised and transferred to the inside covers, the photograph appearing on the back page. Validity continuing for five years and no longer requiring an annual re-validation.

c) Current design, much simplified. The coat of arms incorporates both the Ffestiniog and Welsh Highland titles. The reverse makes provision for the holder's name, address, signature and expiry date. This Card replacing the hitherto separate issue on the Rheilffordd Eryri/Welsh Highland Railway. Residency now described as 'North Wales'.

The Card now costs £2.00 and this rate was certainly was applicable during the currency of a) described above. Residential qualification now defined as Conwy County Borough, Denbighshire, Flintshire, Gwynedd, Anglesey and Wrexham County Borough. One accompanying child travelling free of charge, but requiring a travel ticket. The quarter rate

No · 2110

Festiniog Railway Society

MEMBERSHIP CARD

Available until 31st December, 1989

Not Transferable.   Conditions see back.

Member's

Signature

FRS   FRS   FRS

No 2110   No 2110   No 2110

black print, yellow card, incorporating three detachable vouchers

fares now available in both 1st and 3rd Class.

Discounts on special excursion fares such as Father Christmas trains excluded.

A fare-table dated 20th March 1999 quotes the following –
"Spring Fever. Promotion fare for North Wales residents. Operates on dates advised. May also be promoted as 'Summer Madness' or 'Autumn Gold'. £2.50 per person 3rd Class only. No discounts or free children."
It is known that the 'Spring Fever' offer was available in May 2000.

A quick look at Ordinary Membership Cards. Over the years there have been several designs and different travel facilities on offer. The latter have ranged from free 3rd Class travel, through to three free tickets controlled by detaching a voucher from the Membership Card, and now ten 3rd Class free tickets (1st Class tickets always available at Privilege rates) per annum plus three trips per year for a companion at privilege rates. The current Cards make provision for the recording of these concessions on the reverse by a series of numbers from 1 to 10 plus P1, P2 and P3.

Reciprocal privilege travel arrangements exist with Rheilffordd Talyllyn and Rheilffordd Eryri.

RHEILFFORDD LLANGOLLEN

The first report of a Resident's Railcard appeared in *Journal* (43/1993) announcing the introduction at a cost of £5.00, and affording a 50% discount. Residential qualification being an 'LL21' postcode.

A subsequent report (427/1996) included an illustration of the example now shown, expiry date 31st December 1995. Holders entitlement revised to quarter rate travel, the Card issued free of charge. Pale pink being noted as the colour for 1996, suggesting an annual colour rotation.

LLANGOLLEN RAILWAY PLC

Local Residents Concessionary Travel

Issued to:

Name

Address:

Expires 31.12.1995. Not Transferable.
Must be produced on demand of Railway Staff.
Issued subject to the terms and conditions of the Llangollen Railway PLC.
Not valid on special event dates.
Santa special trains. Berwyn Belle Services.
Please refer to timetable.

black print - pale blue card

The 1995 version of the card (pale blue) was being issued (hopefully with date amended!) during 2000, the discount now $\frac{1}{3}$, apparently adjusted about two years ago.

SEATON & DISTRICT ELECTRIC TRAMWAY

Enquiries reveal that a Resident's Card was introduced some fifteen years ago. Unfortunately there was no provision for a photograph and it was discovered that they were being used in a "transferable" fashion which led to the introduction of the current design three years ago

I think the design of the new card (encapsulated type) is pleasing and further enhanced by the background tram. Qualification is limited to residents of Axmouth, Colyford, Colyton and Seaton affording a discount of "over 60%" on fares. Current cost £2.00 per annum.

(On the subject of tramways, the Matlock Cable Tramway issued Resident's tickets and coupons. In those far off days with a less mobile population perhaps this did not present an entitlement problem. Moving on to the present day The Great Orme Tramway issues Resident's tickets, yet a recent enquiry revealed that a Resident's Card is not used, which would suggest that the good burghers of Llandudno are very honest).

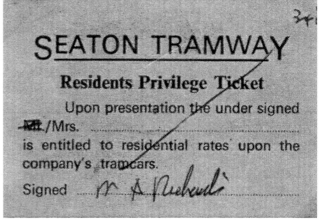

SEATON TRAMWAY

Residents Privilege Ticket

Upon presentation the under signed

Mr./Mrs.

is entitled to residential rates upon the company's tramcars.

Signed

black print - dark green card

SEVERN VALLEY RAILWAY

A report appeared in *Journal* (415/99) mentioning the existence of a Resident's Card. This facility was introduced three years ago. The Card is in two parts, as shown, and costs £5.00 per annum. The holder, together with another adult, entitled to travel at child rates. In addition each adult is allowed to take two children at special rates. Any other children in the party paying normal child fares.

SEVERN VALLEY RAILWAY
Local Residents Railcard

Name ....

Valid until ....

The Bearer, together with one other Adult, is entitled to travel on the SVR scheduled trains at the normal Child rate (about half the normal Adult rate).

Full Conditions of use for SVR Railcards are available from the Company's Bewdley Office.

Membership Secretary

black print - pink card

SEVERN VALLEY RAILWAY
LOCAL RESIDENT'S RAILCARD
(Valid only with an Annual Card)

Name ....

Signature ....

black print - white card

In keeping with other minor railways these Cards are not available on "Santa Specials" etc.

SPA VALLEY RAILWAY
A voucher system is used and an example is illustrated.

Spa Valley Railway

Members Voucher 2000

Voucher exchangeable for one adult return ticket from Tunbridge Wells to Groombridge.

Valid on services up to 1ˢᵗ January 2001 excluding Special Events (consult timetable for details)

black / red print

SWANAGE RAILWAY

Name......................... PHOTO
Number.........................
Valid Till.........................

Signature.........................

CANCELLED

Purbeck Residents Community Card

green print - pale yellow card

SWANAGE RAILWAY
This Card was introduced in 1994 at a cost of £5.00, valid for one year. There has been no change in price since introduction. A discount of 50% is afforded, special services excluded.

WEST SOMERSET RAILWAY
It would seem that this was the first of the Preserved Railways to introduce a Resident's Railcard and was reported and illustrated in *Journal* in 1979 (416/1979, 420/1979), then titled Rail Users Association Membership Card. The Card illustrated had quite a low serial number and was valid until 31st December 1978, suggesting this was the year of introduction.

Sadly it was found that the Cards were being used in a "transferable" fashion which led to a re-design and inclusion of a photograph.

A later reference in *Journal* (83/1983) mentioned a "Starcard" offering a 5p Single and 10p Return reduction to holders. "Starcard" appeared again in *Journal* (198/1998) described as a Resident's Railcard and the description equates with the Card now illustrated. The serial number might suggest an incredible sales figure. Since that report the cost still remains at £3.00 and is valid for three years. I should explain that "Starcard" is the colloquial name.

Residential qualification is limited to community charge payers in West Somerset or Taunton Deane Council Areas, and their children - minimum age 5 years.

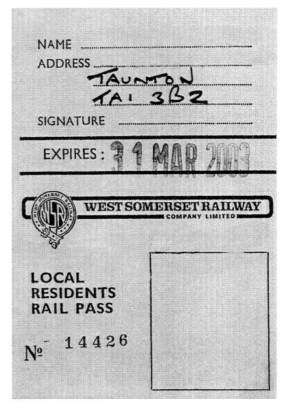

NAME ....
ADDRESS ....
TAUNTON
TA1 3B2
SIGNATURE ....

EXPIRES : 31 MAR 2003

WEST SOMERSET RAILWAY
COMPANY LIMITED

LOCAL RESIDENTS RAIL PASS

N⁰ 14426

black print - pink card

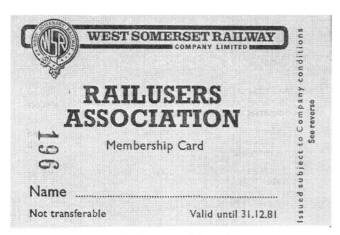

black print - pink card

The holder is entitled to half price adult or child fares on Single, Return or Round Trip Tickets. Rover and other special tickets excluded.

As an aside, the Bluebell Railway told me that they got their idea of a Resident's Railcard from the West Somerset.

BOURNEMOUTH RAIL TRAVEL
The origin of this organisation goes back to 22nd April 1972 when 840 people clamoured for a £1.00 Day Return ticket to London from Bournemouth using special trains. Some charter trains have been run in recent years but privatisation has led to a temporary suspension. A membership scheme commenced 1st January 1994.

A contract with South West Trains allows the pre-purchase of travel tickets at special rates on scheduled service trains to London on selected dates. These are then re-sold to members who must apply by post at least three days before travel. Affording a considerable saving on normal fares. Reduced admission charges are also available to certain London attractions.

Principal Membership costs £5.00 and currently extends to 31st January 2002. A four monthly Newsletter details travel opportunities. Each Principal Membership can apply for up to four Supplementary Membership cards at a cost of £2.00 each but excludes the Newsletter. There is no limit to the number of accompanying passengers but they must travel with the card-holder. Corporate Membership is available for large organisations, minimum number 25.

Travel can only be made on Tuesdays, Wednesdays, Thursdays and Saturdays, and on Sundays once a month. Some peak travel restrictions apply.

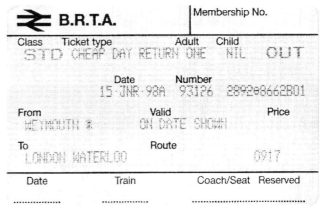

RSP 4599/150

Railcard General Comments

To avoid any repetition it is perhaps convenient to make some general statements that have affected various Railcards over the period of time. The break up of British Rail e.g. sale of Sealink and the subsequent privatisation process have been a contributory factor.

The minimum fare paying age was raised to 5 years from the 17th June 1979.

With effect from 29th November 1981 the maximum age for children's fares increased to 15 years of age.

From 28th June 1984 (368/1984, 456/1984, 372/1987) it became possible to purchase both Family Railcards and Senior Citizen Railcards from Post Offices. The actual Cards can be identified by the inclusion of '(PO)' in the Conditions. Sadly it appears this was not a success and sales ceased from 10th January 1988 (41/1988).

The 12th May 1985 saw some dramatic changes to the fares and discounts applicable to Disabled Persons, Family, Senior Citizen and Young Persons Railcards.

From Mid October 1994 all Young Persons, Senior Citizen, Disabled, Family and Network Cards had an additional 31 days validity added upon renewal. To identify such renewals the Card had to be endorsed on the reverse '31SD' enclosed in a circle. This was to compensate for the railwaymen's strikes during the year.

The policy for replacing lost and stolen Railcards has varied.

In May 1989 a charge of £3.00 was normally made for the issue of a replacement Railcard where the original defaced, illegible or damaged, or where the accompanied photo-card lost. Where a Railcard and/or photo-card stolen or lost in a fire, facts that could be confirmed by the Police or Fire Service, no charge made.

By January 1993 the charge had risen to £5.00.

From the 1st September 1995 a further change "to create customer goodwill and reduce confrontation" at Booking Offices, and "continue to make Railcards successful money making products." Stolen Railcard replacements issued free of charge against a police crime report number/documentation. Expiry date based on information provided by holder – a guess being acceptable.

Lost Cards replaced for a fee of £5.00 but the Railcard Office had to be contacted to confirm issue of the original. Expiry date agreed as in previous paragraph. The Railcard Office carrying out regular checks of customers receiving replacements.

A special Application Form for a Replacement Railcard (RSP 24900) introduced which also served as an indemnity. Travel Agents instructed to refer applicant to a local staffed station. With regard to Disabled, HM Forces and New Deal Cards the holder required to refer to the issuing authority.

From 1st January 1996 the National Conditions of Carriage introduced replacing the former British Rail Conditions. One other feature of privatisation saw the introduction of tickets and stationery forms prefixed RSP (Rail Settlement Plan).

In the same year Railcard leaflets began to appear with a new form of date coding e.g. SN 96A. Version A of the Senior Railcard leaflet for 1996.

A further change was implemented on the 1st June 1997 when the relevant Railcard literature incorporated a 'Receipt of Purchase' to be completed at the time of purchase irrespective of whether a new Card or renewal. By now only one replacement allowed. Those Cards issued in response to special offers sent out with a letter as a form of receipt and this acted as the document of proof.

From 10th January 1999 all Railcard application forms received at stations became part of an audit trail.

From 30th May 1999 Family, Network and Senior Railcards renewable through any Train Company Telesales outlet.

June 2000, Young Persons and Senior Railcard Application and Renewal Forms available on the 'Web'. Details entered on screen and print out obtained.

Conclusion

Unfortunately there are some tantalising questions that remain unanswered, and I have not even covered those Concessionary schemes which also include rail travel.

For the committed Celtic or Newcastle United football supporter *Journal* has reported that Season Ticket holders have been able to obtain travel passes for use when going to and from home games. Whilst the Celtic supporter obtains a free pass, the Newcastle supporter has to pay for the privilege. £30.00 for the 1998/99 season but only £9.75 for 1999/2000 season (344/1995, 184/1998).

Then there are those brief reports in *Journal* that may have involved some form of Membership/Railcard affording cheap travel viz.

Manchester Pullman Club	166/1984
Theatre Rail Club	366/1980, 109/1982
West Midlands Rail Travel Club	488/1985

I would certainly welcome any additional information, criticism or correction, in an endeavour to make the record as complete as possible.

To all those Members of The Transport Ticket Society, both past and present, who have diligently contributed to *Journal* over these many years I dedicate my Presidential Address and this Paper. That information has proved to be a veritable 'goldmine' and I am greatly indebted to them.

I humbly submit that what has been laid before you hopefully justifies the title "It's On The Cards: That Some Things Have Got Worse!"

A personal thank you to *Roger Atkinson, Bill Brinkley, John Britton, Tony Chapman, Phil Drake, Gordon Fairchild, Michael Farr, John Forrest, Robert Forsythe, Roy Hamilton, David Harman, Geoff Hoyle, Brian Hughes, Peter Nichols, Brian Pask, Graeme Paterson-Beedle, Henry Pryer, John Scotford, Paul Smith, Glyn Waite, Martin Warburton,* and *Bob Williamson* who have generously provided a wealth of additional information and tickets.

Also to those Minor Railways and Others mentioned in the text who not only provided tickets, supportive documentation and willingly responded to my many questions.

Before closing I must also thank Andrew Fairholm, for it was he who suggested a research into Railcards in the first place. Little did I realise then where that would lead!

"Thy rod and ..... shall comfort thee".

"Production of Membership Card of recognised Anglers' Club or Association and fishing rod and line .... entitling:-

One Day Returns at Single Fare, or One Calendar Month Returns at 1⅓ Single Fare rounded to nearest 3d."

Railway Clearing House 'Arrangements for Travel at Reduced Fares' Booklet dated 1933.

FAMILY RAILCARD PROMOTIONS

The following list details as many of those known promotions that have occurred since the inception of the Family Railcard. Only a brief outline can be shown hereunder but the *Journal* references will source additional information.

Year	Date	Promoter	Price	Description	Reference
1981	24th May - 7th June		£5.00	Maximum of four adults including card-holder and four children able to travel together for just £5.00	230/1981
	10th May	Sunday Mail (Scotland)	-	Offer comprising a book of vouchers, one of which valued at £2.00 to be redeemed against the purchase of a Family Railcard valid until 30th June 1981.	235/1981
	'Summer' 27th September - 17th October	Western Region	-	Reduced rates available – no details known.	107/1982
		Scottish Region	£5.00	Maximum of four adults including card-holder and four children able to travel together for just £5.00.	107/1982
	1st November -	Pickfords	-	Purchasers of Family Railcards from Pickfords Travel Agencies given a voucher entitling the holder and up to four adults and four children one free 2nd Class journey valid until 12th December 1981.	104/1982, 107/1982
1982	-	Existing Cardholders	-	Reminders sent enclosing a £2.00 voucher (Code 60/203/2).	
	-	Existing Cardholders	-	Reminders sent enclosing a £2.00 voucher (BR 24907/3) to be used as part payment for a ticket bought against new Railcard provided journey taken within one month after expiry of old card.	157/1982
1983	'Spring'	Existing Cardholders	-	Cards due to be renewed during 'Spring' offered a voucher £2.00 that could be used as part payment of a ticket purchased between 1st and 30th June. Also prize draw offer - £20.00 off a Golden Rail Holiday.	318/1983
1984	-	Crawfords Biscuits	-	£6.00 off purchase price of Railcard with 'Pennywise' biscuit products. Voucher obtained through Family Railcard Office at York.	491/1984, 37/1985
	-	International Publishing	-	£6.00 off purchase price of Railcard. Sponsored through various women's magazines and connected to household products. Lasted for one month.	37/1985
	-		-	Holders of Railcards renewed during the year received a voucher (BR 24907/3) exchangeable against an Ordinary Single or Return, Awayday or Saver within a prescribed period. Report suggests this was only a limited offer.	37/1985
1987	January 17th, 24th, 31st, February 7th	'Ready Teddy Go'	£5.00	This appears to have been another group offer but a child carrying a Teddy Bear, or bearing a promotion leaflet for this offer travelled free. Otherwise £1.00 flat fare was applied. Except special services but travel on sleeping cars permitted upon payment of full supplement.	138/1987
1990	15th May - 4th November	Alton Towers	-	Railcard leaflet valid for prescribed period contained a voucher affording the card-holder £2.00 per person off each mixed adult and children group admission (up to a maximum of four adults and four children).	
1991	13th May - 9th November	'Theme Parks'	-	Railcard leaflet valid for prescribed period contained five vouchers for different Theme Parks, basically affording one free ticket. Validity of use varied and not concurrent with leaflet.	
	10th November - 28th March 1992	Disney Home Video	-	£5.00 Voucher towards purchase of Railcard.	
1995	8th January - 23rd September	Sleeper Promotion	-	Accompanying children enabled to travel in 2 berth Sleeper accommodation for a fee of £5.00 (normal rate £25.00)	

Year	Dates	Offer	Type	Description	Reference
1996	29th May - 31st December	'Thomas The Tank Engine'	-	In conjunction with Dillon's Bookshops. A special APTIS card enabling holder(s) to obtain a free 'Thomas the Tank Engine' book valued at £1.99. Also a 25% reduction on any children's books by Hamlyn, Heinemann, Mammoth, and Methuen.	260/1995, 332/1996
1996	August	Walt Disney	-	In conjunction with the film "James and the Giant Peach" a competition for under 11 year olds. The prize a holiday for a family of four in New York. Competition forms were available at cinemas.	
1997	5th January - 31st May	'Travel Back in Time'	-	Two for the price of One' entry to a total of 31 Museums and Exhibitions. For those purchasing a Card during this period offer available until May 1998, for those renewing offer extended for 12 months.	
1998	1st February - 2nd May	Horlicks	-	One million Horlicks jars offering reduced price Railcard plus instant prizes.	
1999	November - January 2000	Connex	-	Free Trial Railcard Mail drop to 300,000 homes in the Brighton, Chatham, Gillingham, Rochester, Faversham, Sittingbourne, Newington and Teynham areas. The pre-printed expiry date either 31st December or 31st January 2000.	88/2000, 142/2000
2000	6th - 26th June	Woolworths	Free Trial Railcard & 25% Discount	Valid for 3 months or 25% off an Annual Railcard. Vouchers valid until 31st July and 30th November respectively.	
2000	1st - 2nd July	Daily Telegraph	Half Price Railcard	Offer valid until 31st July.	

Additional Reference: Article in *Journal* December 1980, page 539 – G. Hoyle

SENIOR CITIZEN PROMOTIONS

The following list details as many of those known promotions that have occurred since the inception of the Senior Citizen Railcard. It should be stressed that certain restrictions and exclusions were applied and varied from time to time. Only a brief outline can be shown hereunder but the *Journal* references will source additional information.

Year	Period	Promotion	Price	Description	References
1980	3rd - 27th November (extended to 11th December)	Go Anywhere	£1.00	Monday to Thursday after 9.30am	513/1980, 541/1980, 31/1981
1981	March	Day Anywhere	£3.00		
	November	Day Anywhere	£3.00		
1982	March	Go Anywhere	£3.00 ¶	Monday to Thursday	154/1982
	November	Go Anywhere	£3.00 ¶		430/1982
1983	May	Take a Friend	-	Within a restricted area of the Eastern Region. An accompanying passenger paying Half Fare on Day Returns only.	320/1983
1984	November	Anywhere within the South East	£2.00 ¶	Monday to Thursday after 9.30am, anytime Saturday and Sunday.	39/1984, 492/1984
	1st - 29th November		£2.00 Single	Monday to Thursday after 9.30am, and anytime Saturday. (accompanied dog £1.00)	492/1984
			£2.00 Return	Monday to Friday after 9.30am, and anytime Saturday and Sunday. (accompanied dog £1.00) The £2.00 returns were only available for travel within areas loosely defined as Scotland, Wales, Cornwall and the South East.	
1985	November	10th Anniversary	£2.00 Day Return ¶	Holders of Day Return Card	486/1985
			£2.00 Day Returns ¶ and reduced rate Savers	Holders of Full Card. £4.00 Saver up to £20.00, £8.00 from £20.10 to £40.00, and £12.00 above. Special A, B and C tickets introduced for this promotion.	
1986	November		¶	same arrangement for 1985.	107/1986, 481/1986
1987	November		¶	Holders of Full Card only. Any day except Friday. £5.00 Saver up to £25.00 and £10.00 above. A and B tickets used.	552/1987, 96/1988
1988	February - June 10th September		£2.00	By paying full Saver fare card-holders could travel 1st Class. Travel anywhere in the Network Southeast Area.	478/1988
	November		£3.00 ¶	Non Card-holding Pensioners upon production of Pension Book. Holders of Full Card only. Any day except Friday. £5.00 Saver up to £20.00, £10.00 from £20.10 to £30.00, and £15.00 above.	571/1988
1989	January	TV Times	(no price details)		95/1991, 144/1991, 330/1991
	November			Any day except Friday. £6.00 Saver up to £20.00, £12.00 from £20.10 to £30.00, and £18.00 above.	508/1989
1990	January			Any Senior Citizen Railcard purchased during the month obtained a 15 month validity.	140/1990
	January	TV Times		Offer of a £6.00 reduction in purchase price.	95/1991, 144/1991
	November			Any day except Friday. £8.00 Saver up to £20.00, £12.00 from £20.10 to £35.00, and £18.00 above.	527/1990
1991	January	TV Times		Offer of a £6.00 reduction in purchase price.	95/1991, 144/1991, 373/1991
1992	27th April - 19th May			Holders of 'Green' Cards offered 50% discount on Savers, Super Savers and AwayBreaks.	240/1992

Year	Date	Promotion	Price	Details	Ref.
1994					101/1994, 138/1994
1995	1st - 27th March / November		£1.00 Off-Peak Ret	50% discount on Savers, Super Savers and AwayBreaks. On the Cardiff Valleys network. Half price (£8.00) card offer.	454/1994
	January / 23rd January -	Post Office Promotion		Birmingham and PTE area, Warwickshire, Derbyshire, Leicestershire, Nottinghamshire, Lincolnshire, Staffordshire, Gloucestershire, Hereford & Worcester and Northamptonshire. Leaflet containing £1.00 voucher valid up to 24th February 1995 towards purchase of a Senior Citizens Railcard.	
	5th - 31st March	Connex South Central/ South West Trains/ Wales & West		Brighton – Bournemouth route, Senior Citizens and an accompanied passenger offered Child rate fares.	
	1st - 14th May	VE Day Commemoration		50% discount in lieu of 34%. Some 30,000 Commemorative Travelcards distributed free to Veteran's Organisations. Tickets marked 'VETERANS' and only to be used by people over 65.	
	28th May - / 23rd September / November	Sleeper Promotion		1st Class Sleeper berth at Standard Class price of £25.00 or £12.50 discounted. Any day except Friday. £6.00 Saver up to £20.00, £12.00 from £20.10 to £30.00, and £18.00 above.	
1997	25th January - / 26th March	Springtime Special	£10.00 Return	To any station on the rail network. Tickets only available by post or telephone from the Raildirect Office, Newcastle Upon Tyne. A mail-shot mainly to the Midlands and North London. An accompanying passenger able to travel for £10.00.	133/1997, 162/1997, 201/1997
	February / End August - / 27th September	Scotrail / TV & Radio Times	£8.00 Return	To any Scotrail station valid for one month. Half price (£8.00) card offer.	133/1997
	4th November - / 14th December	Two for One		Out Tuesday or Wednesday only. Cheap Day/Super Saver, Network AwayBreak, Network StayAway. Promotion notified to 250,000 selected Senior Railcard holders. Advertisements in many publications including TV Times, Radio Times, Readers Digest and Womans Weekly.	
1998	6th - 11th January			Introductory offer in four national magazines. 1/3 off purchase price.	
	March/April	Active Life		Free of Charge Senior Railcard. Card attached to cover of the March/April edition valid until 30.4.98.	217/1998
	1st February - / 2nd May	Horlicks		1 million jars of Horlicks offering reduced price Railcard plus instant prizes.	
	March/May	60th Birthday		Trial mailing to 40,000 prospective customers for their 60th Birthday - about half receiving an offer of £6.00 off the purchase price of a Railcard.	
	18th April - / 30th June			400,000 postcard pack mail-shot to raise awareness of Senior Railcard. No discount offer.	
	June	Help the Aged		50,000 Free of Charge Senior Railcards distributed through Help the Aged outlets. Cards valid until 31 July 1998.	
	21st June - / July	Help the Aged 'Longest Day' Campaign	£7.50 Return	Between any two stations within the f Great Western area. Also available Wales & West, Cardiff Railways, Central Trains, Thames Trains and Virgin Cross Country. Available to any Senior Citizen. Mailshot including a 1/3 off offer.	342/1998

194/1999

	Date	Organisation / Offer	Price	Details
	September			Newspapers, and Magazines offer. A 50% discount travel voucher valid until 31st October for any first time Senior Railcard purchaser. Also a 50% voucher direct mail shot valid until 31st October; to those who previously held a reduced rate Senior Citizen Railcard.
	October	Home & Country		Voucher valid until 30th November. First time buyer of a Senior Railcard able to obtain a card valid for 15 months.
	December - January 1999			A follow up to the previous March/May mailshot to 110,000 people. No price reduction but a free of charge bottle of 50 year old Croft Limited Edition Amontillado when a Senior Railcard purchased. In addition a £1.00 voucher towards the purchase of a bottle of Croft Sherry.
1999	15th February -	First Choice Holiday		By saving up to 4 Senior Citizen rail tickets afforded a discount of £100.00 on a holiday for 2 or more persons. For a single person only two tickets redeemable giving a reduction of £50.00.
	1st - 26th March (except 20th)	Help the Aged and United Nations International Year of Older Persons	£7.50 Return	Between any two stations within the / Great Western area. Also available Wales & West, Cardiff Railways, Central Trains, Thames Trains and Virgin Cross Country. Available to any Senior Citizen.
	June	War Widows(ers) Association		A mail-shot including a £6.00 voucher towards the purchase of a Senior Railcard.
2000	December - 31st January 2000	SAGA and Legion Magazines		Free of charge Senior Railcard valid until 28th February, or until 28th March according to date application received.
	8th April - 5th May	Buy One Get One Free newspaper advertisement		Purchaser required to telephone the Railcard Office to purchase own Card and then obtain another Card free of charge for a relative/ friend provided suitable proof given.
	10th June - 2nd July	Help the Aged 'Stepping Out'	£10.00 Return	Same as March 1999.

KEY   ¶ Up to 4 accompanied children and a dog at £1.00 each.   Additional Reference: Article in *Journal* March 1981, page 101 - G. Hoyle

STUDENT / YOUNG PERSONS PROMOTIONS

The following list details as many of those known promotions that have occurred since the inception of the Student/Young Persons Railcard. It should be stressed that certain restrictions and exclusions were applied and varied from time to time. Only a brief outline can be shown hereunder but the *Journal* references will source additional information.

Year	Dates	Promotion	Description	Journal ref.
1980	June (?) - 31st October	Lloyds Bank	Any student opening a Lloyds Bank account able to purchase a half price card.	
	June (?) - 30th November	W.H. Smiths	14 – 18 year olds able to purchase a Texas Instruments calculator for approximately half price.	
1981	March	Free Return Ticket	Purchasers of Railcard during March able to obtain a coupon for use as a free Return ticket.	158/1981, 192/1981, 91/1983
	June	Validity Extension	Any Railcard purchased from 14th June (until ?) valid for 15 months.	384/1981
	June 14th - 30th October	Lloyds Bank	same as 1980.	
1982	March	Free Return Ticket	same as 1981.	157/1982 91/1983
1983	19th June - 28th October	Lloyds Bank	same as 1980.	
1984	Early January- 18th February	Western Region (Cardiff Division)	Reduced rate travel to any destination. Tickets one piece Edmondsons titled Cardiff Division with originating station as Cardiff (Central) or Cardiff Valley station.	369/1984
1985	September- October	£5.00 Voucher	Purchasers of Railcards during September and October given a voucher valued at £5.00 redeemable against the purchase of a travel ticket.	446/1985
1986	February	Cheap Saver tickets	Reduced rate Savers. £4.00 Saver between £6.10 and £20.00, £8.00 from £20.10 to £40.00, £12.00 above. Special A, B and C tickets used for this promotion.	107/1986
	September - October	£5.00 Voucher	same as 1985.	529/1986
1987	March	Mad March Fares	Travel available for any day except Fridays at discounted rates based on Low Saver fares. £4.00 Saver between £6.10 and £20.00, £8.00 from £20.10 to £40.00, £12.00 above. Low Saver fares costing up to £6.00 sold at applicable discount rates. Special A, B and C tickets used for this promotion.	138/1987, 138/1988
1988	1st March -	£12.00 Voucher	Valid until 31st March 1988. Redeemable against the purchase of an Inter Rail or Inter Rail + Boat Card.	
	13th September - 7th November	Reduced rate Card	Special introductory half price offer £6.00 (£12.00) to new Card holders during this period.	138/1988
	February	Fantastic February Fares	Reduced rate Savers – Fridays excluded. £5.00 up to £25.00 and £10.00 above. Special A and B tickets used for this promotion	139/1988
	1st April -	£10.00 voucher	Valid until 31st March 1989 redeemable against purchase of an Inter Rail Card. Also £30.00 off the cost of an Outward Bound Course booked for any period in 1988 or 1989. £5.00 off normal purchase price (£15.00).	
	11th September - 5th November 1989	Reduced rate Card	Half price offer £7.50 (£15.00) for Cards purchased during this period.	
	29th January - 25th February	Reduced rate Card & Winter Wanderer Promotion	Available to purchasers within period. 50% discount on Blue Saver tickets. Travel on Fridays excluded.	136/1989
	1st April -	£10.00 voucher	Valid until 31st March 1990 redeemable against purchase of an Inter Rail or an Inter Rail + Boat Card. £5.00 off normal purchase price (£15.00).	136/1989
1990	10th September - 4th November	Reduced rate Card		
	16th September - 10th November	Validity extension	Any Railcard purchased between these dates valid for 15 months.	

Year	Dates	Promotion	Description
1991	15th September - 9th November	Reduced rate Card	Half price offer £8.00 (£16.00) for Cards purchased during this period.
1992	13th January - 24th December	Cinema Two for Price of One	Mondays to Thursdays accompanied friend free of charge. MGM, Cannon and Odeon cinemas – initially only available to view seven listed films.
1994	18th September - 12th November	Validity extension	Any Railcard purchased between these dates valid for 15 months.
1995	28th May - 23rd September	Sleeper Promotion	Half price offer (£12.50).
	c. June	Lloyds Bank	Voucher worth £16.00 to purchase a Young Persons Railcard given to students opening an account.
	August	£4.00 and £8.00 Vouchers	Redeemable against the purchase of a Young Persons Railcard. Distribution through Universities & Colleges Admission Service (UCAS) and Student Welcome Packs.
1996	24th May - 11th June	Walt Disney	'Hunchback of Notre Dame' – special train. £1.00 off Official Film Poster (valued at approximately £7.00). Offer also available to Senior, Family, Disabled, HM Forces, Network, Dales, Cornish, Highland and West Highland card-holders.
	mid June - 31st August	Lloyds Bank	Voucher £16.00 - same as 1995. As this voucher had a validity of 12 months and could be in circulation until 31st August the following year, it was agreed that should there be a price increase then the student would not have to pay the difference.
	June - August	British Telecomms	BT Charge Card mail-shot to 400,000 Students starting at University in October. Offer included three month extended validity for purchasers of a Railcard.
	September	£4.00 Voucher	Mail-shot to sixth formers including a £4.00 voucher (valid until 31st March 1997) redeemable against the purchase of a Railcard. Promotion originated from Harrington Dock evidently repeating promotions of previous years.
	1st September - 31st October	Blackwell's Bookshops	Booklet of vouchers issued to Railcard purchaser redeemable at Blackwell's Bookshops. Also available to anyone using a Lloyds Railcard or buying a Railcard with a £4.00 voucher. Promotion supported with radio and press advertising.
1997	17th August	Clubcard	Special 'Branded' Railcard (RSP 4599/189) introduced. Discounts and free offers available during validity of Card. Around a million leaflets used for this promotion.
1998	January - February	Sleeper Promotion	10% off Caledonian Sleeper Fares.
	mid-March	Cinema competition	Participants required to purchase a Railcard and submit entry form, obtainable from cinemas, to Harrington Dock, Liverpool. Free trip to New York and other prizes.
	1st February - 2nd May	Horlicks Promotion	One million jars of Horlicks offering reduced price Railcard, plus instant prizes.
	1st March - 2nd May	Validity extension	Any Railcard purchased given an extra three months validity free of charge. If card not used within the first three months refund available. Three beers for the price of two at certain bars in Scotland included in offer.
	2nd April - 30th June	Validity extension (Scotland only)	Special leaflet sent to 250,000 account holders in April. Any Railcard purchased between dates shown valid for 15 months.
	1st September - 30th November	Carphone Warehouse	Free Railcard to any purchaser of a mobile telephone. Also discounted mobile telephone package for existing Railcard holders.
	c. September	Blinding Offers	Booklet of vouchers issued to Railcard purchasers. Offers included McDonalds, IPC Magazines, Sony Music, Ticketmaster; Carphone Warehouse, Club 18-30 and Firkin Brewery.
	mid December - May 99	£5.00 Voucher	Mailshot to 450,000 students. Special version of the Young Persons Railcard brochure containing an application form to acquire a £5.00 travel voucher from Harrington Dock, Liverpool.
1999	January - 25th February	Ticketmaster	£10.00 voucher to purchase a ticket with a Railcard or towards purchase of a Railcard. Magazine, posters and beer mat advertising campaign.
	25th February - end April	Validity extension	Offering a 15 month Railcard for the price of the normal 12 month version.

2nd April - 30th June	Midland Bank	A quarter of a million account holders targeted with a special leaflet.
August	Leaflet	Offering a 15 month Railcard for the price of the normal 12 month version.
September - October	Freshers Fairs	Mailing to students awaiting UCAS results. Leaflet with offer of a free prize draw of £1000.00 when purchasing a Railcard.
26th September - 14th December	GNER	50% off normal Super Advance Returns with a friend travelling at £10.00 Flat Fare. Travel limited to between 2nd October and 16th December.
27th September - 28th May 2000	Leaflet (YP 99B)	McDonalds, Ticketmaster and First Telecom offers.
1st October - 30th November	HSBC	Leaflet to student account holders including a £5.00 travel voucher redeemable after purchasing a Railcard.
December	Leaflet	Special mailing to parents. 50% including a free draw with a chance to win one of ten Waterstone £50.00 vouchers.
December - May 2000	£5.00 Voucher	Mailing to students. Travel voucher redeemable after purchasing a Railcard.
2000 January - 24th September	Leaflet (YP 00A)	McDonalds, Ticketmaster and First Telecom offers included. Ticketmaster, Times newspapers and First Telecom offers.
8th April - 5th May	Buy One Get One Free	Purchaser required to telephone Railcard Office to purchase own Card and then obtain another Card free of charge for another Young Person provided suitable proof given of age etc.
September - 19th May 2001	Leaflet (YP 00B)	Lonely Planet, Ticketmaster and Times newspapers offers.
October - 5th February 2001	GNER	50% off normal Super Advance Returns and the same for a companion. Not available between 19th December and 3rd January.

Additional Reference: Article in *Journal* May 1983, page 83 – I. Winterflood.

PRICING STRUCTURE

Family Railcard

	single holder	joint holders
wef 17/6/79	£5.00	£10.00
wef 1/3/80	£8.00	£16.00
wef 1/2/81	withdrawn	withdrawn

	single/joint
wef 1/2/81	£10.00
wef 19/6/83	£12.00
wef 12/1/86	£15.00
c May 89	£20.00

Network Card/Railcard

	single/joint	SNR
wef 29/9/86	£10.00	£5.00

		YP/SNR
wef 1/3/87	£10.00	£5.00

	single holder	YP/SNR	joint holders	YP/SNR
wef 12/5/91	£12.00	£8.00	£15.00	£10.00
wef 29/5/94	£14.00	£10.00	£17.00	£12.00
wef 28/9/97	£20.00	withdrawn	withdrawn	withdrawn

Senior Citizen/Senior Railcard

wef 1/4/75	£4.32**	** included VAT @ 8%

	Standard	Cheap Day
wef 1/4/76	£6.00	£3.00
wef 8/1/78	£7.00	£3.50
wef May79 ?	£8.00	£4.00
wef 28/1/80	£10.00	£5.00
wef 19/6/83	£12.00	£7.00
wef 10/1/88	£15.00	withdrawn
wef 7/1/90	£16.00	
wef 17/8/97	£18.00	

Although the above are the standard prices, several local authorities offer reduced rates to Senior Citizens. Some schemes have been around for several years and been reported in *Journal* .

The amount charged for the purchase of a Senior Railcard does vary according to residency. Take for instance the situation existing in the Autumn of 2000.

All District and City Councils in Norfolk and Suffolk offer reduced price Railcards. General cost of a Card £13.50, but sometimes a levy of £1.00 to cover administration. For example Breckland charged £13.50 whilst Forest Heath charged £14.50, the latter including the administration charge.

Comparing this with the Mid Sussex District Council where Cards cost £6.00 (Disabled Persons Railcard £3.50) unless resident in Ardingly, East Grinstead or Ashurstwood where the cost is £4.00. But living in the West Sussex Adur District Council area the resident can claim a £5.00 voucher towards the purchase of the Railcard. In each of these instances the resident has to decide whether to purchase a Countycard Bus Pass, or obtain a discounted Railcard.

Railcards issued under these schemes can sometimes be identified as they bear an issuing authority endorsement stamp and hand dated. Also some are printed in bulk beforehand on an APTIS (or TRIBUTE) machine but will invariably show the normal price.

Student/Young Person railcard

validity	price	minimum fares	
Until 30/6/74	£1.65**	50 pence	£1.00** included VAT @ 8%
Until 30/9/75	?	60 pence	£1.20
Until 30/9/76	£5.40**	£1.00	£2.00** included VAT @ 8%
Until 30/9/77	?	£1.25	£2.50
1/10/77 – 30/9/78	£7.00	£1.50	£3.00
15/9/78 – 30/9/79	£7.00	£1.75	£3.50
15/9/79 – 30/9/80	£8.00	£2.00	£4.00
1/9/80 – 30/9/81	£10.00	£2.00	£4.00
14/6/81 – 30/9/82	£10.00	£2.00	£4.00
wef 4/10/82	£10.00	£3.00	£.6.00
wef 19/6/83	£12.00	£3.00	£6.00
wef 10/1/88	£15.00	£3.00	£6.00
wef 7/1/90	£16.00	£3.00	£6.00
wef 6/1/91	£16.00	£4.00	£8.00
wef 11/1/93	£16.00	£6.00	£12.00
wef 17/8/97	£18.00	£6.00	£12.00
wef 26/9/99	£18.00	£7.00	£14.00

SCHEDULE OF FORMS MENTIONED IN THE TEXT AND THOSE KNOWN TO BE RELATED TO RAILCARDS AND PROMOTIONS (excluding Minor Railways etc)

Ref	Form	Type	Colour	Notes
BR 1919/12	Railcard Wallet	plastic	clear	inscribed Railcard
BR 1919/19	Railcard Wallet	plastic	red and green	inscribed Student Travel - two versions seen
BR 1919/21	Railcard Wallet	plastic	clear	inscribed Railcard
BR 1919/57	Railcard Wallet	plastic		
BR 35884	12 Month Season Ticket		blue	1st and 2nd Class
BR 3588/9	Photocard		red	portrait and landscape versions
RSP 3588/9	Photocard		red	landscape
BR 3588/14	Young Persons Photocard	16/23 version	blue	introduced 1st March 1987
BR 3588/14	Young Persons Photocard	pictorial	mauve	
RSP 3588/15	Young Persons Photocard	multi-advertisement	orange	introduced 17th August 1997
RSP 3588/16	Young Persons Photocard	pictorial	orange	introduced 29th September 1998
RSP 3588/17	YP Temporary Permit to Travel	pictorial	orange	introduced 9th January 2000
BR 4402/164	Daily Mirror - Daily Record Voucher	valid until 11/9/76	black print	One Free Awayday Child ticket
BR 4402/192	Rail Riders - Voucher		red/blue/black	value £1.00
BR 4402/192	Rail Riders - Voucher		red/yellow/black	value 50p (APT design)
BR 4402/192	Rail Riders - Voucher		not known	value £1.00 (APT design)
BR 4403/177	Heinz Promotion – Voucher	valid until 31/3/79	not known	value £5.00
BR 4524/14	Rail Europ Senior Citizen Railcard		red	
BR 4524/14	Rail Europ Senior Railcard		red	
BR 4524/21	Inter Rail		blue	
BR 4524/21	Inter Rail		brown	cover inscribed 'under 26 years of age'
BR 4524/23	Rail Europ Junior Card		blue	
BR 4524/38	Inter Rail		brown	
BR 4536/1	Network Card Day		red/blue	11th April 1987 - Adult and Child versions
BR 4536/1	Ian Allan Network Bonanza		red/blue	24th October 1987 - Adult and Child tickets inscribed "Network Card Holder"
BR 4536/1	Network Gold Card Christmas Bonus		green/red/blue	December 1987

NCR 51

Ref	Form	Colour	Notes
BR 4556/1586	Minimum Charge - Single/Return	red	later prints have either Student Railcard or Young Persons Railcard added
BR 4556/1702	Senior Citizen - Flat Fare	red	
BR 4556/1704	Special Promotion - Flat Fare	green	
BR 4563/14	Child Awayday Return	red	
BR 4563/15	Child Weekend Return	red	

INTIS

Ref	Form	Colour
BR 4576/1240	Minimum Fare - Single	red
BR 4577/484	Minimum Fare - Single (RV)	red
BR 4578/1240	Minimum Fare - Return	red
BR 4578/1584	Special Promotion - Flat Fare	green
BR 4579/484	Minimum Fare - Return (RV)	red

APTIS

Ref	Form	Colour	Notes
BR 4599/15	Supplement	black	} used for 1st Class Network Card upgrade
BR 4599/15	Supplement	pink	}
RSP 4599/15	Supplement	pink	}

Form	Card	Type	Colour	Notes
BR 4599/17	Senior Citizen Railcard		mauve	introduced 10th January 1988 concurrent with the withdrawal of the CHEAP DAY CARD
BR 4599/17	Senior Citizen Railcard	negative SCR background	brown	
BR 4599/17	Senior Citizen Railcard	positive SCR background	brown	
BR 4599/17	Senior Railcard	pictorial	brown	introduced circa October 1988
BR 4599/17	Senior Railcard	pictorial	green	introduced May 1990
RSP 4599/17	Senior Railcard	pictorial	green	introduced 5th January 1992
BR 4599/18 #	Senior Citizen Railcard	CHEAP DAY RETURNS	green	withdrawn 10th January 1988 (# Duplicated form number - also appears on the reverse of the Voyager Railcard – 'pseudo APTIS' version)
BR 4599/19	Family Railcard	pictorial	green	withdrawn 14th May 1990
BR 4599/19	Family Railcard	pictorial	blue	introduced 15th May 1990
BR 4599/19	Family Railcard	pictorial	brown	introduced 29th May 1994
RSP 4599/19	Family Railcard	pictorial	brown	withdrawn 29th May 2000
RSP 4599/19	Family Railcard	pictorial	brown	pre-validated either until 31/12/99 or 31/1/00. Given an APTIS form number in error (Connex promotion)
BR 4599/20	Young Persons Railcard	16/23 version	red	introduced 1st March 1987
BR 4599/20	Young Persons Railcard	pictorial	blue	
BR 4599/20	Young Persons Railcard	pictorial	mauve	introduced circa September 1992
RSP 4599/20	Young Persons Railcard		mauve	
BR 4599/21	Annual Season Ticket Holders Rcd		green	withdrawn from 8th October 1988
BR 4599/22	Network Card	pictorial	blue	
BR 4599/22	Network Card	pictorial	orange	
RSP 4599/22	Network Card	Network SouthEast	orange	introduced 12th May 1991
BR 4599/23	Day Rover		blue	
BR 4599/24	Gold Card		gold	
BR 4599/24	Annual Gold Card	pictorial	gold	
RSP 4599/24	Annual Gold Card		gold	
BR 4599/25	Gold Card Duplicate		gold	
BR 4599/25	Annual Gold Card Duplicate	pictorial	gold	
RSP 4599/25	Gold Card Duplicate		gold	
BR 4599/26	Gold Capitalcard		gold	
BR 4599/27	Gold Capitalcard Duplicate		gold	
RSP 4599/27	Gold Travelcard		gold	
BR 4599/66	Annual Gold Travelcard	pictorial	gold	
BR 4599/66	Annual Gold Travelcard		gold	
RSP 4599/66	Annual Gold Travelcard	pyramid	gold	
RSP 4599/66	Gold Travelcard Duplicate		gold	
BR 4599/67	Annual Gold Travelcard Duplicate	pictorial	gold	
BR 4599/67	Annual Gold Travelcard Duplicate	pyramid	gold	
RSP 4599/67	Gold Travelcard Replacement		gold	
BR 4599/68	Annual Gold T'card Replacement	pictorial	gold	
BR 4599/68	Annual Gold T'card Replacement		gold	
RSP 4599/68	Annual Gold T'card Replacement	pyramid	gold	
RSP 4599/68	Annual Gold T'card Replacement		gold	
BR 4599/69	Network Card	Gold Card Partner	blue/gold	a version exists with an all gold border
BR 4599/77	Cornish Railcard		purple	
BR 4599/77	Cornish Railcard		turquoise	
BR 4599/79	Highland Railcard	map version	mauve	BR Logo omitted on one version
RSP 4599/79	Highland Railcard		mauve	
BR 4599/81	Gold Card Dup Encoding Exchange		gold	

Form No.	Card	Type	Colour	Notes
BR 4599/81	Gold Card Replacement		gold	
BR 4599/81	Annual Gold Card Replacement	pictorial	gold	
RSP 4599/81	Annual Gold Card Replacement		gold	
BR 4599/82	Gold Capitalcard Dup Encoding Exchange		gold	
BR 4599/92	Frequent Traveller	Saturday	dark grey	
BR 4599/93	Frequent Traveller	Weekend	dark grey	
BR 4599/94	Frequent Traveller	un-restricted	dark grey	
BR 4599/145	West Highland Railcard		blue	
RSP 4599/145	West Highland Railcard		blue	
BR 4599/150	Bournemouth R.T.A.		white	
RSP 4599/150	B.R.T.A.		white	also a later version titled B.R.T.
BR 4599/155	Surrey C.C. Authority Card		brown	
RSP 4599/155	Surrey C.C. Authority Card		brown	
BR 4599/163	Family Railcard	pictorial	yellow	'Thomas The Tank Engine' promotion 29/5/95 - 31/12/95
BR 4599/170	Dales Railcard		plum	
RSP 4599/173	Peterborough Card		dk blue	valid from 10.00am
RSP 4599/173	Peterborough Card		dk blue	valid from 9.30am
RSP 4599/183	Esk Valley Railcard		green	
RSP 4599/188	Network Railcard	pictorial	sky blue	introduced 28th September 1997
RSP 4599/189	Young Persons Railcard	multi-advertisement	orange	introduced 17th August 1997
RSP 4599/197	Senior Railcard	pictorial	purple	introduced circa early 1998
RSP 4599/204	Senior Railcard	pictorial	purple	Active Life Promotion valid until 30th April 1998. Pre-validated, given an APTIS form number in error.
RSP 4599/206	Seniors Railcard	Valley Lines - pictorial	blue	
RSP 4599/216	Student Railcard	Valley Lines	blue	
RSP 4599/217	Young Persons Railcard	pictorial	orange	introduced 29th September 1998
RSP 4599/234	Surrey C.C. Student Fare Card		brown	
RSP 4599/244	Prism Weekend Pass		bright pink	
RSP 4599/252	Heart of Wales Line Railcard	pictorial	grey	two versions exist - one has a white reverse the other orange, introduced 29th May 2000
RSP 4599/253	Family Railcard	pictorial	orange	
RSP 4599/254	Surrey C.C. Student Fare Card		blue	
RSP 4599/255	Surrey C.C. Student Fare Card	DUPLICATE	grey	
BR 4889/1	Voyager Railcard		blue	form number BR 4599/18 also appears on reverse
TRIBUTE				
RSP 7599/19/SCT	Family Railcard	pictorial	brown	withdrawn 29th May 2000
RSP 7599/24/SCT	Annual Gold Card		gold	
RSP 7599/25/SCT	Annual Gold Card Duplicate		gold	
RSP 7599/66/SCT	Annual Gold Travelcard	pyramid	gold	
RSP 7599/67/SCT	Annual Gold Travelcard Duplicate	pyramid	gold	
RSP 7599/68/SCT	Annual Gold Travelcard Replacement	pyramid	gold	
RSP 7599/81/SCT	Annual Gold Card Replacement		gold	
RSP 7599/188/SCT	Network Railcard	pictorial	sky blue	
RSP 7599/197/SCT	Senior Railcard	pictorial	purple	
RSP 7599/217/SCT	Young Persons Railcard	pictorial	orange	
RSP 7699/253/SCT	Family Railcard	pictorial	orange	two versions exist - one has a white reverse the other orange, introduced 29th May 2000
BR 24881	Student Identity Card	valid until 30/6/74	red	
BR 24881	Student Identity Card	valid until 30/9/75	green	

Form No.	Card	Detail / Validity	Colour	Notes
BR 24881	Student Railcard	valid until 30/9/76	dark brown	
BR 24881	Student Railcard	valid until 30/9/77	purple	(example seen with no starting date)
BR 24881	Student Railcard	valid 1/10/77 - 30/9/78	yellow	
BR 24881	Student Railcard	valid 15/9/78 - 30/9/79	mauve	
BR 24881	Student Railcard	valid 15/9/79 - 30/9/80	dark brown	
BR 24881	Student Railcard	valid 1/9/80 - 30/9/81	blue	
BR 24881	Young Persons Railcard	valid 14/6/81 - 30/9/82	red	
BR 24881	Young Persons Railcard	open validity	red	introduced 1st March 1987
BR 24881	Young Persons Railcard	16/23 version	blue	introduced circa September 1992
BR 24881/1	Conditions	pictorial	mauve	incorporating ten Travel Request Forms
BR 24881/1	Conditions	valid until 30/6/74	black	
BR 24881/1	Conditions	valid until 30/9/76	black	
BR 24881/1	Conditions	valid 1/10/77 - 30/9/77	yellow	dated January 1978
BR 24881/1	Conditions	valid until 30/9/78	yellow	
BR 24881/1	Conditions	valid 15/9/78 - 30/9/79	red	
BR 24881/1	Conditions	valid 1/9/80 - 30/9/81	blue	dated May 1981
BR 24881/1	Conditions	valid 14/6/81 - 30/9/82	red	dated July 1982
BR 24881/5	Voyager Railcard	plastic card	red	dated May 1984
RSP 24881/5 **	Student Railcard	Midland Bank	red/black	(** Duplicated form number) 4 year validity - an HSBC titled card exists (not seen)
BR 24889	Senior Citizen Railcard	valid until 31/3/76	blue	
BR 24889	Senior Citizen Railcard	valid until 31/3/77	blue	
BR 24889	Senior Citizen Railcard	open validity	red to mauve	
BR 24889	Senior Citizen Railcard	negative SCR background	brown	security grid horizontal or diagonal
BR 24889	Senior Railcard	pictorial	brown	introduced 10th January 1988 - withdrawn 14th May 1990
BR 24889	Senior Railcard	pictorial	brown	introduced May 1990
BR 24889	Senior Railcard	pictorial	green	pre-priced £10.00 BR/TV Times - August/September 1997 promotion
BR 24889	Senior Railcard	pictorial	green	introduced 5th January 1992
RSP 24889	Senior Railcard	pictorial	green	pre-priced £8.00 Half Price Offer - January 1995 promotion
BR 24889/1	Conditions		blue	undated (valid 1976 - Jan 1977)
BR 24889/1	Conditions		red	dated January 1978
BR 24889/1	Conditions		red	dated January 1982
BR 24889/3	Gift Token		green	value £4.00 - circa 1980/81
BR 24889/4	Senior Citizen Railcard	DAY RETURNS ONLY	red	valid until 31/3/77
BR 24889/4	Senior Citizen Railcard	DAY RETURNS ONLY	green	security grid horizontal or diagonal - withdrawn 10th January 1988
BR 24889/5	Conditions		green	dated November 1980
BR 24889/6	Gift Token		purple	value £8.00 - circa 1980/81
BR 24898	Family Railcard	valid until 29/2/80	lt blue	
BR 24898	Family Railcard	valid until 28/2/81	red	
BR 24898/1	Family Railcard	valid until 28/2/81	red	overprinted 'TWO'
BR 24898/5	Family Railcard Photocard		blue	overprinted YORK (C/O) 'TWO'
BR 24898/7	Family Railcard	valid until 28/2/81	red	overprinted 'ONE'
BR 24898/9	Family Railcard		green	overprinted 'TWO'
BR 24898/10	Family Railcard		green	overprinted YORK (C.I.O.)
BR 24898/10**	Family Railcard	pictorial	blue	(**Duplicated form number) introduced 15th May 1990 - withdrawn 29th May 1994

Form No.	Card	Validity	Colour	Notes
BR 24898/10**	Family Railcard	pictorial	brown	(** Duplicated form number). Introduced 29th May 1994.
BR 24898/11	Conditions		green	undated
BR 24898/12	FR Temporary Photocard Auth'y		green	undated
BR 24898/13	FR Temporary Photocard Auth'y		green	also has 'BR11' on front
BR 24898/14	Application for a Rcd Replacement		green	two part form
RSP 24900	Senior Citizen Railcard	Beverley B.C.	white/pink	
BR 24902			orange/black	
BR 24903	HM Forces Railcard	valid until 31/12/82	blue	A serial - Army
BR 24903	HM Forces Railcard	valid until 31/12/87	blue	A serial - Army. Validity later extended to 31/3/89
BR 24903/1	HM Forces Railcard	valid until 31/12/82	blue	N serial - Navy
BR 24903/1	HM Forces Railcard	valid until 31/12/87	blue	N serial - Navy. Validity later extended to 31/3/89
BR 24903/2	HM Forces Railcard	valid until 31/12/82	blue	AF serial - Air Force
BR 24903/2	HM Forces Railcard	valid until 31/12/87	blue	AF serial - Air Force. Validity later extended to 31/3/89
BR 24903/3	Conditions		not known	
BR 24903/4	HM Forces Railcard	valid until 31/12/89	brown	validity later extended to 31/1/90
BR 24903/4	HM Forces Railcard	valid until 31/12/90	red	validity later extended to 31/1/91
BR 24903/4	HM Forces Railcard	valid until 31/12/91	purple	pictorial - validity extended to 31/3/93 using a silver sticker, and accepted up to 30/6/93
BR 24903/4	HM Forces Railcard	valid until 31/3/94	brown	pictorial - validity extended to 31/3/95 using a silver sticker, and accepted up to 30/4/95
BR 24903/4	HM Forces Railcard	valid until 31/3/95	brown	pictorial - accepted up to 30/4/95, extended with a gold sticker until 31/3/97 (accepted up to 30/4/97). Re-validated with a silver sticker up to 31/3/98 and later accepted up to 30/6/98
RSP 24903/4	HM Forces Railcard	valid until 31/3/98	blue	pictorial - validity extended to 30/6/98
RSP 24903/4	HM Forces Railcard	valid 12 months from …	brown	(revised 1998 version)
RSP 24903/4	HM Forces Railcard	valid 12 months from …	brown	(revised 2000 version)
BR 24903/5	HM Forces Photocard			colour identical to the accompanying Railcard
BR 24903/6	Conditions		brown	contemporary with BR 24903/4 - valid until 31/12/89
BR 24903/6	Conditions		black	valid for period 1/1/92 - 31/3/93
BR 24903/6	Conditions		black	valid for period 1/4/93 - 31/3/94
BR 24906	Disabled Persons' Railcard		brown	overprinted YORK (C.I.O.)
BR 24906	Disabled Persons Railcard	pictorial	brown/blue	'bird' design - overprinted C.I.O. YORK
BR 24906	Disabled Persons Railcard	pictorial	brown/blue	'bird' design - overprinted C.I.O. YORK - pre-priced £12.00
RSP 24906	Disabled Persons Railcard	pictorial	brown/blue	'bird' design - overprinted DPRO NEWCASTLE
RSP 24906	Disabled Persons Railcard	pictorial	brown/mauve	'bird' design - overprinted DPRO NEWCASTLE
RSP 24907	Senior Railcard	pictorial	purple	introduced circa early 1998
BR 24907/3	Voucher		orange	value £2.00 valid 1/3/82 - 31/3/82. Issued BRHQ Family Railcard Office.
BR 24907/4	Voucher		green	value £1.00 valid until 31st March 1983, Journey Club Railcard offer.
BR 24907/6	Inter Rail Discount Voucher	valid until 31/3/88	lt blue/red	value £12.00
BR 24908	Journey Club Railcard	valid until 31/12/82	green	Annual Season Ticket Holder's Card
BR 24908	Journey Club Railcard	open dated	green	Annual Season Ticket Holder's Card
RSP 24908**	Network Railcard	pictorial	sky blue	(**Duplicated form number). Introduced 28th September 1997.
BR 24908/1	Journey Club Railcard	valid until 31/12/82	red	'Nominee's Card'
BR 24908/1	Journey Club Railcard	open dated	red	'Nominee's Card'
BR 24908/2	Conditions		green	dated September 1981
BR 24908/2	Conditions		red	dated November 1982
BR 24908/4	Journey Club Railcard	valid until 31/12/83	green	Annual Season Ticket Holder's Card
BR 24908/5	Journey Club Railcard	valid until 31/12/83	red	'Nominee's Card'

Reference	Item	Type	Validity / Issuer	Colour	Notes
BR 24908/7	Journey Club Leaflet			red/green print	dated September 1984
BR 24908/8	Annual Season Ticket Holder's Rcd			orange	introduced 24th May 1998
BR 24909	New Deal			yellow/orange	
BR 24909/15	Travel Key Ticket	1st Class		not known	
BR 24910/3	Cornish Railcard	Adult		gold	
BR 24910/4	Cornish Railcard	Child		blue	
RSP 24911	Senior Railcard			purple	Help The Aged Promotion. Pre-validated and valid until 31/7/98
BR 24912	Network Card		pictorial	blue/red/grey	
BR 24912	Network Card		pictorial	orange	pre-priced £15.00 - dual holder
BR 24912	Network Card		pictorial	orange	pre-priced £17.00 - dual holder
RSP 24912	Network Card		pictorial	orange	pre-priced £17.00 - dual holder
RSP 24912**	Disabled Persons Railcard		pictorial	green	(** Duplicated form number) overprinted DSPRO NEWCASTLE – introduced end 1998/early 1999
BR24912/1	Network Card		pictorial	blue/red/grey	overprinted DISCOUNT
BR 24912/1	Network Card		pictorial	orange	pre-priced £10.00 - dual holder
BR 24912/1	Network Card		pictorial	orange	pre-priced £12.00 - dual holder
BR 24912/2	First Class Supplement			blue	£1.00 upgrade
BR 24912/5	Network Card		pictorial	orange	pre-priced £8.00 - single holder
BR 24912/5	Network Card		pictorial	orange	pre-priced £10.00 - single holder
BR 24912/6	Network Card		pictorial	orange	pre-priced £12.00 - single holder
BR 24912/6	Network Card		pictorial	orange	pre-priced £14.00 - single holder
BR 24912/7	Network Card		pictorial	orange	unpriced - single holder
RSP 24913/A	Senior Railcard		pictorial	purple	valid until 28/2/00 - SAGA/Legion Magazines promotion
RSP 24913/B	Senior Railcard		pictorial	purple	valid until 28/3/00 - SAGA/Legion Magazines promotion
BR 34236	Manchester Rail Travel Club		valid until 31/12/80	red	
60/203/2	Travel Voucher		Network SouthEast	red	value £2.00 valid 1/3/81 - 30/4/81
41043	Travel Voucher		validity variable **	blue/red	value £3.00 - issued by Marketing Manager NSE HQ. ** Example seen valid until 31/5/91
CAS/PO36668A	Travel Voucher		validity variable **	green	value £2.00 issued by Senior Citizen Railcard Office. ** Example seen valid for the period 1/11/86 - 30/11/86
CC252717	Personal Network Day Voucher		Network SouthEast	red/blue/grey	valid for Network Card-holder and up to 3 Adults (£5.00 Flat Fare each) and up to 4 Children (£1.00 Flat Fare each) for any Saturday or Sunday between 12/10/91 and 17/11/91
CC310662A	Personal Network Day Voucher		Network SouthEast	red/blue/grey	valid for Network Card-holder and up to 3 Adults (£6.00 Fht Fare each) and up to 4 Children (£1.00 Flat Fare each) for and Saturday or Sunday between 10/10/92 and 15/11/92
EU200GS1LPARKGNSP	Travel Voucher		validity variable **	red/grey	value £2.00 issued by Network SouthEast HQ. ** Example seen valid for the period 2/2/88 - 1/3/88
RSPNSDR001	Dales Railcard			plum	pre-priced £10.00 Agency issue

Items without Form References:

Item	Validity	Colour	Notes
Manchester Rail Travel Club	valid until 31/10/7-	lt blue/gold	} both examples of these tickets current during the 1970s
Manchester Rail Travel Club	valid until 31/10/—	red/gold	
Manchester Rail Travel Club	valid until 31/10/—	black/gold	
Great Rail Club Membership Card		red	plastic card (APT design)
Great Rail Club Voucher	circa 1979	red/blue	value 50p (APT design)
Rail Riders Membership Card		red/yellow/black	plastic card (APT design)
Rail Riders Membership Card		red/blue/black	plastic card
Student/Young Person Railcard Voucher	valid March 1981	blue	free Return ticket

Card	Valid	Colour	Notes
Monthly Train Pass	valid 1/11/81 - 12/12/81	yellow	booklet valid between September 1981 and 30th April 1982
Pickford's Family Railcard Voucher	circa 1981	not known	free Return ticket
Senior Citizen Railcard Gift Token		red	
1st Class Executive Rail Card	valid until 31/8/82	yellow	plastic card
Travel Key		orange/black	
Journey Club Voucher	valid until 30/9/83	red	free Day Return Ticket
Network Day Rover - Adult	13th September 1986	red/blue	the reverse includes an offer of a £4.00 reduction in the purchase price of the newly launched Network Card / withdrawn 25th October 1986
Lancashire Senior Citizen Rail pass		red	value £10.00
Inter Rail Discount Voucher	valid until 31/3/90	blue	plastic card
Intercity Frequent Traveller	early 1990 - 9/5/91	black/red	
Strathclyde Resident's Card	1992 - 31/3/96	orange/black	
Great Eastern Network Card	c mid 1994	not known	
London Tilbury & Southend Network Card	c mid 1994	not known	
Thames Trains Tripcard	valid until 24/9/94	not known	
Thames Trains Tripcard	valid until 27/5/95	blue	
Great Eastern Discovery Card	September 1995	not known	
Great Eastern Holiday Special Card	c August 1995	not known	
Great Eastern Sports Saver	end 1995	not known	
Blackwell's Bookshop		black/mauve	promotion booklet valid September 1996 - April 1997
Rail Readers Loyalty Club - Intercity	valid until 31/8/97	grey/red	plastic card
Virgin Cross Country First Day Club Card	valid 6/1/97 - 31/1/98	red/black	plastic card
South Kent College Discount Card	valid 8/9/97 - 3/7/98	not known	
Anglia Commuter Club		green/purple/brown	
Rail Readers Loyalty Club - Virgin Trains	valid until 31/8/98	black/red/yellow	plastic card
Virgin First Day Club Card	valid 1/1/98 - 31/12/98	not known	plastic card
f Great Eastern Weekend Travel Pass	valid 1/1/98 - 31/12/98	blue/white	plastic card
f Great Eastern Companion Card	valid 1/1/98 - 31/12/98	blue/white	plastic card
Central Trains Matchmaker Card	valid 2/1/98 - 30/4/88	not known	
Welfare to Work Railcard	introduced 6th April 1998	not known	
Blinding Offers		orange	only available in Scotland
f Great Eastern Annual Season Ticket & Companion Card	valid 1/1/99 - 31/12/99	blue/white/green	promotion booklet valid until 30/9/99
'Get Up & Go Card'		not known	plastic card
f Great Eastern Summer Saver Card	valid 1/3/99 - 31/12/99	orange/yellow/blue	plastic card
f Great Eastern Destination Weekend	valid 10/7/99 - 30/9/99	blue/yellow/green	plastic card
Rail Readers Loyalty Card - Virgin Trains	valid 1/1/00 - 31/12/00	tan/red	plastic card
Connex Loyalty Card	1/2/00 - 31/12/00	blue/yellow	plastic card
Island Residents Discount Card	Autumn 2000	orange/yellow	Stagecoach Island Line
South West Trains - Gold Service		blue/gold/white	free Weekend Travel ticket (landscape version)
South West Trains - Gold Service		blue/gold	free Weekend Travel ticket (portrait version)
Cornish Photocard		green	